Dating the Single Mom

WHAT WOMEN NEED TO KNOW
AND WHAT MEN NEED TO DO

By
Ayesha Goodall & Co.

Table of Contents

Acknowledgments

This book is a compilation of real-life stories from 7 amazing women and 1 courageous man regarding their dating journey as a single mom and as a man dating a single mom. Thank you all for saying yes and co-authoring this amazing book with me.

I am so grateful to God for planting the drive and courage in me to stand up and be a voice for single moms globally. I thank God for guiding me into my calling to help other women like me to stand up and be courageous enough to band with me in sharing their journey in this area of their lives, which in turn serves as a massive movement to impact the masses of single mothers who feel hopeless.

I am so grateful for my 3 children and their unconditional love. I also give thanks to my mother for inadvertently instilling me, the relentless spirit to go after everything that I desire. I thank my deceased father, Levon Vines for being truly authentic in who he was in my life, which has molded me into being an authentic soul. I want to thank my Bonus Dad, Blaine Young, for teaching me the lesson and being the example of what the different faces of abuse looks like. I gotta thank my uncles on both my mom's side and dad's side, you keep me grounded about how to survive in these streets when the going gets tough.

I want to give a special thanks to my ex-husband, Ruben Goodall, for co-creating and blessing us with such wonderful children. I cannot forget to thank my eldest daughter's dad, Wayne Conwell, for helping me co-create such a beautiful soul of a daughter. If it weren't for these men, I wouldn't be the woman I am today. I am truly blessed.

I want to give thanks to all my male mentors, near and far for pouring into my soul life and success principles. Instilling me the importance of personal development and becoming the best version of myself. Thank you for allowing me to borrow your belief in not only being a success in business, but also in love.

Believing that I *am* love, I deserve love, and that I could love again. These beliefs I have now adopted and made them my own.

All my male friends who truly are just my buddies, my pals, thank you for accepting me as I was and who I have grown into. Thank you for the talks about men and how men think and move. Even though I didn't listen at times, trust me, I heard those voices even if it were after the fact.

Ron M. Stone, you have been a blessing, a thorn, and a joy at the same time. Thank you for taking this journey with me on this project. Thank you for your patience.

David Burrus, you have been a huge inspiration from the time we met in April 2014 when we spoke on the same stage. I knew, at some point, we were going to do some work together. Look at us now; you have written the Foreword in my book. Thank you for your incredible contribution.

Last and definitely not least, I must give a gi-normous thank you to the beauty behind this framework, my publishing team KS Media and Publishing, Adrienne E. Bell. Words cannot express the amount of gratitude that I have for you, THANK YOU.

Thank you all who advocate and support my book and movement. I know you will enjoy this ride in reading about *Dating the Single Mom*.

Dedication

This book is dedicated to single moms globally. Single moms who have lost their hope in finding love, despite having children.

I dedicate this book to the young ladies who desire to become mothers. This is a tool that they can use to educate them about what it takes to successfully choose their purpose partner and how to collect data while dating before having children. Also, educating them regarding the consequences of making poor choices when it comes to dating and having children.

For my men out there who are either single with no kids or single dads dating single moms, this is for you. A guide you on how to properly study a woman with children before taking on the journey of dating/courting them. Dating single moms is a multifaceted concept. This doesn't mean just taking them and their children on, it means *learning* and *considering* that they have experienced various degrees of hurt, trust issues, juggling their masculine and feminine energies from having to take on the responsibility of mom/dad and many other psychological and emotional dynamics. There is nothing wrong with any of this when you are transparent about your intentions up front, and she is transparent with hers, you are both on the same page and pursuing personal growth and healing from past traumas.

This book is for the village raising our young ladies and young men. **Each one, teach one.**

This beautifully authored book will change the trajectory of single moms by leading them to heal within, nurture their children, and equip them to build the confidence needed to love and find love again.

Dating the Single Mom: What Men Need to Know, and What Women Need to Do

Foreword by: David Burrus

I am not sure if you are old enough to remember life before smartphones and GPS, but for many of us, we can recall having to use maps and handwritten directions to get from point A to point B. There was once a time when you would have to call and get directions from someone, if you were looking to arrive at a certain destination and a particular time. If your memory dates back long enough, you can even recall stopping by the local drug store or gas station to get a map that would help you navigate your way to your desired location. Things were so much more simple then, yet they were absolutely complicated at the same time.

We are living in a day and time where many are searching high and low for a map, directions, or even some form of a GPS to help them navigate their relationships from point A to point B. The frustration seems to be arising, because there are no such things. Enter Ayesha Goodall, and this incredibly timely piece de resistance, entitled **Dating the Single Mom**.

What you will find in the next few pages of this remarkable masterpiece of a book is the GPS… The map… The directions… That you have been so desperately seeking for navigating your relationships as single moms, or with single moms. Ayesha has taken her mastery of parenting, her experience in singleness, as well as her rich network, and has merged them together to coordinate this collection of stories and experiences from some very qualified ladies and gentlemen.

The real genius of this book is Ayesha's ability to create a platform for other key subject matter experts to share their perspective on dating the single mom. Gentlemen, prepare to have your mind blown by the richly profound and precise insight that will be shared with you from and for the man's perspective. What you will discover is an unbiased account of how a responsible man walks with and does life with a single mother, and her children. What you are about to discover will absolutely revolutionize the way you handle a woman and her children.

What you are about to discover is that *Dating the Single Mom* is a very well-balanced book. Just as the men will discover what they need to know to successfully date the single mom, women will gain priceless insight on how to successfully date *as* the single mom. The next few pages are infused with wisdom, insight, and perspective that will inform your narrative and give you the wisdom you need to date as a single mom. The perspectives that the contributors of this book have shared will open the eyes of both men and women, and will undoubtedly lead to more fruitful and productive dating experiences.

Cheers to Ayesha Goodall for this incredible offering. *Dating the Single Mom* is transformational, and will serve you and those connected to you for years to come.

"It's time to stop dating and start collecting data as you move forward in your purpose with your life partner!"

- AYESHA

The Unveiling

By: Ayesha Goodall

L adies, ladies, ladies, and gentlemen; let's have an honest chat about one of the most divisive issues when dating: *The Single Mom*. I have a few things to get off my chest, and I encourage you to keep an open mind and heart while reading this. Let's be honest, there's a negative stigma surrounding single mothers in the dating world, and I don't like it. We're judged, looked down upon, and shown no mercy when it comes to men and relationships. There are many different reasons why I want to address a few concerns and share my perspective. Most importantly, I pray I provide every single mother and every single man reading this with hope and helpful tips on navigating intentional dating.

I am the author of a book called, *The Single Mom Survival Guide: Moving on with Life After Divorce.* That book was for the women that had experienced divorce, newly divorced, and women that experienced break-ups with men they had children with. I wanted to share a bit about my personal story. I struggled in my marriage and eventually trusting when it came to dating again. I didn't feel like there was light at the end of the tunnel, and I wanted to tell my story to give women hope in similar situations.

Dating *as* a single parent is just as challenging as raising children. Single mothers tend to be engulfed in the lives of their children. So much so that we lose ourselves. We no longer pay attention to our needs and wants. We have other people that count on our attention and focus. We sweep our personal lives under the rug and begin living vicariously through our children. It happens so quickly and unnoticeably that by the time we look up, the kids are adults, and we're left trying to find the life we left behind.

Many single mothers will wait until their children become 18 and/or are off to college before entertaining just the *idea* of dating. But I'm here to tell you that you don't have to deprive or deny yourself love for years on end just because you're a single mother.

In the beginning, we all have this "Ken Doll" idea of what we want our man to look like. We think he should come to us in specific packaging. But that's just not reality. It's much more complicated than that. I had daddy issues, so I had a rough introduction to relationships with men. As I aged and had some experiences of my own with men romantically, I learned that a man could not give me what I was supposed to find within. Happiness, wholeness, and confidence, are virtues you should possess before asking or wanting a man to add to. You cannot be empty or lacking in self-worth, self-value, self-respect, or self-love and expect a man to come in and fill in the holes. It doesn't work that way.

I had to realize that I had a lot going on, on the inside. Not only did I have daddy issues, I had issues with my mother and just about every man I'd dated thereafter. Honestly, I have to say my biggest problem wasn't just the men that I was attracting or dating. The problem was me. That's right, I said it! *Me*. The first time I got married, the marriage lasted for 3 months. I never wanted to admit that I didn't know what I was doing. I had no idea why I was married. I discovered that I had made an irresponsible decision, so I got out. I realized that I needed to rediscover who I really was, *alone*.

My second husband and I dated for six months before we got married. He and I had dated before in our early 20's. That marriage lasted three years. The pain of a second divorce and being a single mother again was excruciating. I'd always keep a handful of platonic male relationships. My father was not as present but my uncles were pretty good at staying connected with me. Needless to say, I'd been exposed to men and how they operate from a very young age. I saw quite a bit. So when my ex-husband began acting up, I was able to diagnose exactly what was going on. At one point after my divorce, I felt defeated. I wasn't so sure that there was someone out there for me. My divorce left me with such a bad taste in my mouth about men. As time moved forward, so did my way of thinking. I unearthed an interesting fact about myself; I wasn't fully developed emotionally. Being aware of your pain is the first step, addressing it is the next.

When I was newly divorced, I was shut down from men. I didn't want anything to do with them. I had to get to know me all over again. I needed to care for me, love me, and find out who I was in this new chapter of my life. I was evolving and I needed to learn how to embrace myself as a whole. I learned about my quirks, dislikes, and insecurities. Not only did I come to know these things, but I also came to love those same flaws that I disliked. I had to learn how to give myself the same grace I gave to others. Over time, I became secure with who I was.

You have to date yourself. Get to know who you are from the inside. Get to know your true self; your inner child. Get to know what works for you. Dedicate yourself to growth. Reevaluate your social circle. Forgive yourself. Get comfortable with being single. Spend time with yourself. Dote on you. You deserve that. And take as much time with yourself as you need to heal and find acceptance.

I had to ask myself some questions during the process of transition like, *what do I want out of my life? What do I want to accomplish?* I wanted to ensure the best possible results in the next relationship I decided to commit myself to. You're only going to get what you give yourself. But what you give you, has to be positive reinforcement. I wanted men to see me from a different lens. I wanted them to be able to see that I was focused on my success and my children. I wanted them to know that I *wanted* a man, I didn't *need* one.

I remember when I met a gentleman that I respected as a mentor. He knew my story and knew that I was anti-men. He was a married man but we began dating. Although his marriage was on a downward spiral, it was still a setup. It's no secret that more times than not, someone gets hurt in situations like this. Simply put, it's just not smart to get caught up in a married man. They can spend all the money they have, send you on trips, and whisper sweet nothings but it still won't amount to anything in the end because more than likely they won't divorce their spouse. More than likely they will go back to their spouse, leaving you to pick up the pieces. Now just for the sake of conversation, let's just say the married person you're dating actually does divorce their spouse to be with you; the likelihood that infidelity will be a problem in your relationship is too high. That's too much wounded energy and brokenness trying to come together. It's not worth the heartbreak.

Everyone has an innate need to love and be loved. But marriage? That's a separate subject. If you're a single mother out there dating, be clear on what it is you're looking for and don't settle or make excuses for why you can't have what you want. Being a single mother isn't a curse or a dark cloud over you, it just means you have to go about dating differently. And that's okay. A lot of single moms share the belief that because they have children, they're doomed to a life of being single or that no man will want them. Be very cautious with the beliefs that you adopt because they manifest into mindsets and ultimately behaviors. Once you've ingrained that belief within yourself, you'll spend a lot of time trying to unravel that same belief. Do yourself a favor and be kind to yourself. Be open to the possibility of getting what you want. Fill yourself with positive and optimistic thoughts.

As the process continued for me, there was still a small percentage of me that still had *daddy issues*. My father was a street guy, involved with gangs and drugs. He once told me that my mother gave him an ultimatum: **family or the streets**. He chose the streets and later admitted that he wished he would have made a different decision. But it was too late. By the time he realized that he'd made a mistake, I was an adult woman with daddy issues manifesting in my relationships with men. There was a lot of unfinished business between my mother and my father, especially my father and I. Although I'm sure my father's decision to give up his family for the streets was hurtful for my mother, she never kept me away from him. As an adult now, I know my father did the best he could. But his decision made me feel abandoned and made it hard for me to trust men. His absence made me an independent person and in a sense, I wanted to be led, from a fatherless daughter's perspective. So deep down, I looked for men that could lead me.

My stepfather was a good provider but he was a terrible husband and stepfather. He was abusive physically, mentally, and emotionally to my mother. He was present but he was no real father to me. It seemed like he wanted me to take the place of his own daughter. When I was 16 years old, he asked me if I would change my last name to his last name, which was only a knee-jerk reaction to his own daughter never taking his last name. Personally, I felt like that was disrespectful to my own father. I declined and that pissed him off so bad that he slammed me against a wall.

I did have some positive male figures in my life along the way. My grandfather was one of them. That man loved me entirely and I knew that. He gave me whatever I wanted and made sure everyone else did too. Some of my fondest memories were of falling asleep in his lap. In those moments, I felt safe and protected. He took good care of me and showered me with love. I'm sure he had his ways because we all do but he was never inappropriate with me. I also had an uncle, Chester who was a father type figure to me. He loved me similar to how my grandfather did.

The issues that I had with my mother were totally different than the issues I had with my father. A mother is a role model for her daughter. A mother shows her daughter who she's supposed to be. A mother is a teacher and a friend, a confidante. But my mother struggled with her own personal issues. She didn't love herself. Due to that, we always had a strained relationship. I was the star child of my family. I was very close to both my grandparents and very much so the favorite grandchild. My mother couldn't understand why. When I became an adult, my mother's best friend came to me and told me the truth about my mother. She said that my mother was always jealous of me and she couldn't understand that part about her. That tidbit of information was mind-blowing. I didn't understand it either. But I started looking into what she shared with me. I noticed that all I wanted to do was please my mother. I'd been chasing her all my life to have a relationship with her. I wanted her acceptance. I wanted her love. But the truth is, how could I expect her to give something to me that she hadn't really given to herself. It's impossible. I couldn't let her lack thereof, be my reality. I had to live for me and find a way to love myself in spite of her not showing me how to do so.

My mother and I had a very abusive relationship. Well, she was abusive to me. She would beat me senseless sometimes. But she didn't stop there. Abuse doesn't work that way. Usually, when you abuse someone, it's in more ways than one. So it wasn't just the physical abuse that was damaging but she was also emotionally abusive. She'd do things like call me out of my name and belittle me. Until one day when I was 17 and decided to give her a dose of the truth. I told her that she was the devil and that she hid behind religion because she did. She taught me a lot, but in some areas, I was much more mature than my mother.

Not only did I have trust issues with men but more importantly, I had a difficult time trusting myself. I didn't trust my own feelings and my own intuition. I had to learn how to trust myself. I had to understand that there was something inside me that was attracting the same kind of person. I didn't quite know what it was so I had to explore that. Oftentimes, our healing is done in layers. Just as soon as we think we're past an issue, there's another one to resolve.

At one point, I was working with a life coach and she asked me to make a list of the qualities I valued in a man. She also asked me to be realistic about what it was I was looking for. She placed emphasis on being realistic because oftentimes women jump into relationships without knowledge of what they truly want, then become devastated when the relationship goes south.

Of course, you'll kiss a few frogs before getting to your Prince. However, as I grew in my personal development, I began to meet men that were truly groomed to treat women well. That's when my perspective began to change drastically. My hope was revived. I began to invite the possibility of a future with someone. Two years after my divorce, I became soft to the idea of dating so I put myself on a timeline. I gave myself until my son was 5 years old, to start dating. I wanted my son to be at an age where he could articulate what he felt about anyone I was dating.

I started dating someone when my son was about 5 ½ years old. When I met this man, I dated him for 90 days. During this time, he showed me everything I didn't want in a man. I gave him 3 more months just to see if things would take a different turn. To my surprise, the man I was dating came to me and told me that I was a beam of light and he was dark. On top of that, he had issues with his mother. This time around I was a lot more conscious and intentional with dating. I'd been single and worked on me. I knew what I wanted. Subsequently, I was able to identify what I wanted and not sit in a relationship for any extended period of time waiting and hoping for things to get better. My kids loved him, but after 6 months of dating I cut him off. We did a good job of keeping our issues in the adult realm and not allowing our issues to be seen by the kids and affect them. However, I knew that if I continued the relationship, my unhappiness would be unveiled. I couldn't allow that to happen. To this day, he and I are still friends.

When my son was 8-years-old he came to me with some big requests. He told me that he wanted a father and a family. Essentially, he was tired of being alone too. At the time, I too wanted companionship. So I mutually understood him. I had to have a conversation with him and explain that yes, I was single but I was looking for someone who was a good fit for me *and* him. I wanted a man that could teach my son foundational life skills, how to be a man, etc. I wanted a man who wasn't looking to live off of me. I wanted someone who wasn't abusive in any way. I needed to identify what worked for both of us because he and I are a packaged deal. I wanted to enjoy my journey to finding love too.

Remember ladies, dating is supposed to be fun; not one boring interview after another. Ask questions? Yes! But make it enjoyable. Truly take the time to get to know a person. Set boundaries and hold your standards high, so that you are able to separate the men that are worth your time and those that aren't.

Appearance is everything when dating. Be mindful of the message you are putting out there based on how you're dressed. Let's be very honest here, a man will treat you how you present yourself. If you want a man's respect and full attention, don't give him too much else to pay attention to. No matter what kind of man you're dating, they all respond to the physical aspect of a woman the same. So dress the part. Be tasteful.

More times than not, women with children are always looking to date for the sole purpose of a budding relationship. Which is completely understandable. But a lot of us don't find dating easy. A lot of us don't even know how to date. None of this is a reason to feel shame. Just look at it as a learning opportunity. Moms, be careful of this. Mommy mode is a default setting. But it's not your job to mommy a man. We have to remember that these are adult men that we're dealing with, that have their own pain and their own crosses to bear. We have to keep in mind that when he comes home at night and takes off his suit and outer world persona, he's looking for love, not a mom. Unless you're dating a mama's boy. It's important to identify what kind of man you're involved with. It's equally important to pay attention to the background and upbringing of your potential mate. Not everyone is cut from the same cloth and a person's family largely contributes to who they are at the core and what they value. I found that men that don't have positive relationships with their mothers tend to have a difficult time in relationships with women.

I've come to the conclusion that there are **<u>3 types of men</u>**:

The Independent Man: knows how to balance his relationship between his woman/wife and his relationship with his mother

The Broken Man: still needs his mother to mommy him and wants a woman to do the same

The Withdrawn Man: not close to his mother at all and hasn't healed from the wounds of his broken relationship with her

Dating with intention is important. You have to know what you want going in and clearly communicate what it is you're looking for. This will save you in the long run. The art of communication is a big deal when getting involved with someone romantically. Do you know how to engage with a man? And I don't mean sexually. Do you know how to be a friend to him? What impression would you like to leave him with? Ask yourself questions like this so that you become more intentional. Also, be mindful of the pitfalls when dating. Women have to shift their mentality when dating so you don't come off as desperate or needy.

<u>3 things I want women to stop doing when you're out there collecting data, aka dating:</u>

1. playing the victim
2. projecting feelings about unhealed issues onto new relationships
3. acting out of desperation

Nothing will send a man running in the opposite direction than those 3 listed actions above. On the flip side, there are some things you can do to ensure the possibility of new love.

1. **Ask conversational questions.**
2. **Determine what level of dating you want to entertain.**

One of the most important things to focus on as a single mom is collecting data, not so much about just dating. I'm not saying to go in and interrogate the guy. Remember, keep it light, fun, and intriguing. You may ask, 'what is the difference between dating and collecting data'?

Dating can be flighty and endless when you are not dating intentionally. There are a lot of women and men that just date for fun, date multiple people at a time, or date just to pass time. I call these people 'serial date mongers.' As single moms, we don't have time. We make time for dating, especially because we WANT to. When collecting data, we have purpose, we have a goal in mind. We want to know that the person we are collecting data from is aligned with our purpose, with our thinking and they have us in mind as a total package including our children. I'm not saying look for someone to take the place as the children's father, that can be a deterrent for many men. Collecting data is about asking the right questions. Show interest in him as a person. Get to know his hobbies, his favorite color, favorite movie then move into finding out what his childhood was like, find out his love language. In the formative stages make it mentally stimulating, interesting, leave him wanting and looking for more meaningful conversation. Before diving deep into this collection, always start out with sweet and simple dialogue to help keep the mood relaxed and easy, which will allow him to open up to you. It's time to stop dating and start collecting data as you move forward in your purpose with your life partner!

Ladies a lot of time we give up too much too soon. What I mean by that is we talk too much and set ourselves up by coming off too needy, desperate or weird. Allow him to talk, listen with intent. How does he feel about children? Does he have children? How is his relationship with his mom and the women in his family? His circle of friends? Get to know his psychological side. Look to see if he has an open mind for change and growth. Find out if he is a God-fearing person and if he truly loves himself. In knowing that he will eventually love you and your children the same way.

Please do not throw these things upon him all at once on the first date. You want to show that you're interested in getting to know him, not be interesting. A man will take the lead a lot of the time in the conversation if he is an evolved man or in the midst of his evolution. Set timelines. Set out a schedule. Create balance and keep your children the priority, always.

I hope to encourage single mothers to do the necessary self-work first. Make sure that you're loving yourself first, and have done the inner work to attract the love you're looking for. When I decided to become a better person, my life changed. I began seeing life from a more positive and optimistic perspective. Since discovering the happier side of life, I decided I wanted to reach other mothers with my new-found knowledge and hope. I wanted them to understand that they could accomplish anything they wanted to but that belief could only come from within.

Again, healing may come in layers. Be open to the possibility of true self-love and complete healing. Counseling is key and surrounds yourself with people that you can truly connect with and elevate you. If finances are an issue and going to a therapist isn't feasible, there are so many self-help books that would definitely assist you in your process. Again, this is going to be difficult. But you have children that are looking up to you that are going to mimic your behavior and take on some of your personality. Who do you want to be? What kind of children do you want to raise? You have to be committed to yourself and your healing more than you've been committed to burying the hurt. I mean, what's the alternative? You stay the same and ultimately get the same result.

You will not be able to engage in any healthy relationship when you have unresolved issues and open, unhealed wounds. It's just not possible. To the single mother out there battling the residue of daddy issues or mommy issues, go seek help. I can't stress that enough. That's a big part of working on yourself. Resolving those issues is a part of the healing process and the road to true inner freedom. There's no way you should try to settle deep-seated issues alone. There's help available and taking advantage of it would be the wise decision. It will be challenging, but a healthy challenge evokes healthy change. You will cry. You will have to uncover things that you buried long ago and you will have to face the ugliness. But unless you dig up those issues at the *root*, you'll continue to have the same issues. Band-aiding the problems doesn't make them go away. That's only a way for you to ignore the problems until they grow and manifest yet again. Childhood trauma is like a planted seed. It grows as you grow. When you dig up the root, there's a hole left there. You'll feel raw at that time. Be careful during this time because you may be inept to fill that hole with the same negativity that you just worked so hard to get past. You should fill the hole with self-love, self-acceptance, self-care, and self-respect. This is called the journey to being whole. This is where you are working with God to fill the voids. **You will never settle or sell yourself short when self-love is a core value.**

"It's okay to be an alpha woman, just hang your balls up when you get home!"

~Tona Phillips

He's Just Not That Into You

By: Tona Phillips

When it comes to dating and men, I wasn't taught a lot about what was unacceptable or what I should allow. It was more of a, *'she'll learn on her own.'* I'm on a mission to help single women to stop blindly dating! It's time that we unveil our truths, secrets, and lessons learned to one another so that we can stop falling victim to bad relationships and poor choices in men.

I grew up believing that women should be the one who caters to her mate; that we should know and play our position. There is a universal law that women are supposed to be more caring and be the emotional reservoir for the relationship. I took that and ran with it! Due to that poor advice, I suffered dearly. Believing that advice had me giving the world to each man I dated even though he didn't deserve it. I found myself in relationships that were unbalanced and unsatisfying to me. At the time, I didn't know that it was dissatisfaction that I was experiencing, let alone had the ability to articulate it. I've recently come to that conclusion. In the past, I approached men. I no longer do that. I had to learn that I'm the flower to be picked. I had to learn how to be more feminine. I was quite masculine in how I approached dating and interacting with men. I got attention from them, but I wasn't meeting *quality* men. I had to learn how to communicate what I wanted. Before I could even think about getting into another relationship, it was more important for me to learn who I am on a deeper level and what it is I truly want.

It was 2001 when I met my daughter's father, Paul, while in college. I was attending Alabama State University in Montgomery, Alabama. I wanted to be a physical or occupational therapist, but I discovered my talent to do hair while I was in college. He approached me one day and asked if I could braid his hair. He then gave me his number and wanted **me** to call **him** to do his hair, which made no sense! Normally, a client contacts me to get *their* hair done. He was setting the stage for me to chase him. **Red flag**. I called him for a week straight before I was able to get in contact with him and he finally came to get his hair done. The weekend after I'd braided his hair was Valentine's Day. He showed up at my place with flowers and a teddy bear. We were a couple from that moment forward. There was no dating, no questions, and no friendship ahead of the relationship. I just accepted the flowers and teddy bear as if it was good enough. I didn't know any better at the time.

During my time in college, Paul and I moved in together. I was in love with him. I trusted him, and I thought he and I would always be together. While living there, I'd gotten pregnant, and he was very supportive at the time, but we miscarried. At the beginning of the relationship, I was making more money than he was. He was all about making sure home was taken care of. So I gave him the responsibility of making sure the bills were paid, and he seemed to like that. I can't say I know he was in love with me because he didn't say it, but I felt his love through his actions. He always showed his affection through gestures. (i.e., cards, flowers, etc.) He was also very protective of me. When students would try to play like they couldn't pay for their hair appointment, he would basically shake them down for the money.

One time, my best friend came to visit me from California. She flew into Atlanta and we drove there to pick her up and brought her back to Alabama. When we got back to my place, we had plans to go out. Before we did, I told her I had to *ask* Paul if I could go out. She gave me the most puzzled look. She said, "Ask?" She saw the red flag before I did. I didn't see his control as control. I saw it as protection.

By the end of my four years in school, I determined I didn't want to be a doctor anymore. I wanted to be a cosmetologist full-time. I'm from California and Paul was from Chicago. I'd planned to move back home and invited him to come along with me. He wasn't quite ready when I asked so he went back home, and so did I. We were apart for 6 months when I called him and told him I missed him and wanted to see him. I was on my way to a hair show and asked him if I could stop in Chicago to see him on the way to the hair show. We agreed to meet up. I was excited to see him but I wasn't ready for what happened next. Things had gotten hot and heavy. We started kissing when one thing led to another and we ended up having sex that night. Immediately after we finished, he grabbed my hand and said, "Let's pray." At first, I thought it was a bit odd since it was bad timing, but the real shock was the actual prayer itself. It went a little something like,

> 'Thank you gracious Father for life and all that you give us
> We pray that Tona is not pregnant and we can continue
> life the way it is. Amen.'

Before he could barely finish the prayer, I snatched my hand from his and asked, "You don't want a baby with me?" He said, "I don't know." I specifically told him to make sure he had condoms before I arrived. In my opinion at the time, it was his responsibility to make sure we didn't have unprotected sex so whatever happened was on him. When I left, I was pretty pissed but I still loved him. He made me feel like I shouldn't have slept with him that night. I went home a week later and noticed that my cycle was late. I called and informed him that I was late and might be pregnant. Immediately he denied the possibility of the child being his. He felt that because we lived in different states, he couldn't have been the one responsible for my pregnancy. We'd been pregnant twice before and I miscarried. I believe he felt that because there was a lot of distance between us, I probably had another man back home. But pregnancy happens the same way it always has and it was ignorant for him to believe he couldn't have been the father. Everything seemed fine until I said I was pregnant.

I went through the entire pregnancy alone. He was still living in Chicago and I was living in California. He called around the 8th month of my pregnancy and said he was coming to visit me. When he arrived, he was shocked to see that I was actually pregnant. During the visit, he decided to move to California but still wanted a DNA test. It seemed like he categorized me as the kind of woman who had multiple sex partners and lied about what I was doing and who I was doing it with. I wasn't that woman. Yes, I'm an attractive woman and confident in who I am. Yes, I have a lot of male friends but I wasn't sleeping with *any* of them. I took my time with men and some men have a hard time digesting that kind of truth from someone they assumed the worst about.

When he moved to California my family welcomed him with open arms and of course, everyone wanted to know, *when are you two getting married?* My family was persistent about asking him about marriage and they felt like it was a justified question since he'd moved to California from Chicago and we now had a baby. I understood their thought process and reasoning for asking that question, but I believe it had a counterproductive effect on him. I don't think he truly wanted to get married. I think he felt pressured. I believe he also did it thinking that was the only way he could be a full-time father to our daughter. These were all the wrong reasons to get married.

I had my daughter in 2005 and I'm sure you know what it is like to get your body back to what it once was after giving birth. Paul became extremely verbally abusive repeatedly telling me how bad I looked. Sometimes, I'd fall asleep on the couch and he'd tell me that I needed to stop sleeping on the couch because I was putting dents in the cushions. I was wondering what he expected my body to look like seeing as though I'd just had a baby. He said he wanted me to be a size 7. I didn't know where he got that from because my regular size was a 12/14. When a man judges a woman in this manner, it plants seeds of self-doubt. It's best to leave when they start this behavior rather than wait until you're sucked in losing self-confidence with every ugly word. If I'd truly respected myself, I would've left Paul the first time it happened.. Again, I didn't know any better and chose to stay with him.

One weekend in 2007, we decided to take some time for ourselves. My friends watched the baby and we headed to San Diego for an India Arie concert. After the concert, we walked along the beach, he proposed, and I said, "yes." We were engaged for one year before I started asking questions. Every time I asked him about planning the wedding, he was nonchalant about it. He'd tell me, "When I figure it out, you'll be the first to know. Don't worry about it." I didn't know why he couldn't just answer the question. In hindsight, he always showed classic abuser behavior. I just hadn't caught on to it while it was happening.

In 2007, I'd just gotten my cosmetology license and that was a huge accomplishment for me. I was extremely happy and he seemed indifferent about it. When he showed his lack of interest in my accomplishment, I knew we were going to have problems moving forward. Any time I wanted to discuss my hair career, he displayed the same emotional distance. It even seemed like he wanted to sabotage my career. Anyone that does hair knows that the busiest day of the week is Saturday and he didn't want me to work on Saturdays. He wanted me to be at home with our daughter. I told him no and suggested that my parents could watch her on Saturdays if necessary. He felt like that was me throwing my responsibility as a parent on my parents. We went back and forth on that for a while before I gave in. Afterward, my income decreased significantly as I knew it would. But that gave him even more control. Anyone that truly cares for you will show you the support you need and clap for your achievements. Make a mental note of when they don't.

My father was in prison for 10 years and he was released the same day I obtained my license. He was sick with a condition called Trigeminal Neuralgia causing him to have constant migraine headaches lasting at least 24 hours. When he was released from prison he also had stage four cancer of the lymph nodes. My father and I were close and his relationship with Paul was friendly. My father was the only person in my family that Paul would talk to but he kept everything very superficial. He never told my dad the truth about us. My dad saw everything from a different perspective. He took a neutral stance and told me that Paul was confused and advised me to be patient with him.

We were having problems and I wanted to go to couples therapy but like many men, he was against it. He felt like nothing was wrong with him, therefore any kind of counseling would be a waste of time and money. Although he had daddy issues that he was never willing to discuss, I never pushed it but secretly hoped he'd change his mind. I learned the hard way that you can only fight for a relationship when there are 2 willing participants. I can admit he's a great father even though his father wasn't. For that reason, I never wanted to come between him and our daughter. I wanted them to be close. They both deserved unconditional love.

My ex always chose the extreme route as a resolution to all of his problems with me and our daughter. When it came to making us 'pay' for his pain, he knew *exactly* how to do that. His mother was abusive towards him which explained his dislike for women in general. When my daughter was about 2 years old, I had a conversation with his mother. She told me to be careful with my daughter because her father was a bad child. I told her that I didn't have those problems with my daughter. She went on to tell me that she had to beat him with a belt every day for a year. I was shocked as I listened in disbelief. She admitted to abusing with so much pride. I was hurt for him. Oddly, he loves his mother very much. However, I learned in therapy that oftentimes, the abused loves their abuser no matter what. His mother was also abused by his father and his younger siblings' father. It seems like abuse is all he knows.

He carried that same abuse with him into his adulthood. He was a man that loved to threaten people. I determined that was his way of exerting control, possibly because he was never in control as a kid. He learned that the only way he could be in control was to scare others into doing what he wanted. When we were together, we had a dog that he would beat with a belt, in the face, while being tied to a door, for peeing on the floor. This kind of behavior definitely made me afraid of him.

One day I came home from work and Paul wasn't there. I called him to see where he was and he told me he was on his way home. I walked into the kitchen and noticed a receipt on the floor. I picked it up, looked at it and saw it was a receipt for flowers. So I jumped in the shower and made sure I smelled good for him since I thought he had flowers for me. When he got home, he was empty-handed. I waited an hour and approached him and asked, "So where's my flowers?" *His face dropped.* He went on to tell me that he bought some flowers for a sick co-worker. I *knew* it was a lie. I began watching his behavior and noticed that he wasn't coming straight home after work. He'd say he was going to play basketball and wouldn't come back home until midnight. There was a pattern. It was obvious that he was cheating. Since he wasn't looking to put any effort into our relationship and he was unhappy enough to step out on me, I decided to reel my emotions back in. I never checked him about what I noticed because it was only confirmation for my suspicion.

Paul and I were having a lot of issues and each day the relationship was changing for the worst. I immediately thought that sex would be the fix. At the time, we were living in Burbank, CA which is a predominantly caucasian area. A lot of my girlfriends were caucasian women. One of them threw a sex party and I attended, hoping to learn some new tricks to take home. When you initially walk in the party, you're given a name tag with an alias. Everyone there is to be called by the name on their name tag. My name was 'Sweet Puss.' I mingled with the ladies there and noticed one lady's name was 'Sally Swallows.' I joked with her asking does Sally actually swallow and out of nowhere the music stopped. All the women there looked at me and said, "who doesn't?" They asked me to sit down and we went through an exercise of how to properly give fellatio. When I got home, I tried to show him what I learned and he turned me down. I was shocked! He said he didn't want to have sex until we were married. I was confused because we were living together and just had a baby. That's when I realized things between us were indefinitely different. That's when I realized I'd given the relationship my all, but he wasn't there *with* me. He was physically there in the flesh but his mind was somewhere else. We never got married. The relationship dysfunction carried on for another 2-3 years before I told him that we needed to do something different.

One day we had a disagreement and things were escalating so I decided to take a walk and gather myself. When I came back I couldn't get into the house. He'd locked the door. I was knocking on the door asking him to open it. He made me wait outside for 10 minutes before he opened the door. He told me that because I left I wasn't welcomed anymore. I went to take a walk because I was tired of fighting with him. In my eyes, we were breaking up. If I stayed, I'd only be delaying the inevitable. I found out that Paul was secretly removing my name from the bills, including the lease for the house. When the lease was up, he renewed the lease but removed my name. One day, the electricity bill came in the mail which was a bill that was in my name. When I noticed the bill came in with just his name on it, I asked him about it. He said he was doing it for 'credit' purposes. I didn't know it but he was setting the stage for me to leave.

In 2009, we officially broke up. When we decided to go our separate ways, we sat down and had a conversation about our daughter. At the time she was attending a school that integrated deaf students into all classes. She was learning sign language during her stay at that school. She was doing well and we didn't want to uproot her amid the school year so we agreed that she would stay with him for the remainder of the year and move back with me when the school year was over. When the time came, he conveniently forgot that we had that conversation and disappeared with her. I didn't have access to my daughter for months. He kidnapped her and told her that I'd abandoned her. Till' this day, she still lives with him and I'm going through a terrible custody battle. Ladies, when making agreements with the father of your children, it may sound strange or unnecessary, but get everything in writing. Verbal agreements are inadmissible in court. All this time, I thought my daughter's father and I were on the same page and we definitely weren't.

After we went to court, we finally came to a visitation agreement. He had her during the week and I had her on the weekends. One Sunday evening, I was looking to drop her back off to him, but he wasn't home. I immediately sent him a text message asking him to let me know when he was back home and I'd take my daughter and my godson, who was riding along, to 7-11 while we waited for him to arrive home. Five minutes later when we arrived at 7-11, I received a text message reply from him saying that he was home. Not even a minute later, he was pulling up at the store and started making a scene! He snatched my daughter out of my car and we got into a verbal altercation from there. I got out of the car and told him he didn't need to be that rough with her. Things got physical when he pushed me towards the car and held me there. I didn't like how dramatic he was being and I wasn't fond of how he was handling my daughter or me. On top of that, he had a new girlfriend that was also there at the time this happened and she inserted herself in the situation which made everything worse. I hadn't seen this woman a day in my life! I looked at him, shocked that he was allowing this woman to get involved. I called the police because I wanted the incident to be documented. Ten minutes later the police arrived and arrested ME! I asked what I was being arrested for and the officer told me, "domestic violence." I made bail and the next day we had a custody court date.

At the time, my lawyer determined it wasn't a good idea for me to have an open custody case *and* domestic violence case at the same time. He advised that I agree to whatever terms Paul wanted and focus on clearing up the domestic dispute. So I signed a contract that basically said I relinquish my parental rights. At the time, I didn't understand the legal jargon in the contract so I just signed it. I believe that altercation was his way of gaining a foothold over the situation. He wanted the control and he had that. Due to the arrest, I had to attend court-ordered domestic violence and parenting classes.

Going to therapy and attending the classes is what saved me from being sad and depressed. I still felt a sense of guilt for leaving her with him even though it was completely out of my control. But my hands were tied and there was nothing I could do about it. While attending the classes, I learned so much about domestic violence. I once thought that domestic violence was just sexual or physical. No, it's also emotional, financial and a few others. I had no idea I was a victim of domestic violence during my relationship with Paul. I grew up in South Central, Los Angeles. It's a rough area to grow up in and all of our dysfunctional behaviors are normalized, so we are oblivious or we overlook the long-term effects it has on us.

After everything that happened with the domestic violence incident, the case was thrown out. But I still had to finish the classes. Once the classes were complete, I thought I would be able to focus solely on being a mother. Little did I know I was about to encounter the next hurdle....*the girlfriend*. Paul's girlfriend was constantly sticking her nose where it didn't belong. My daughter was my and Paul's responsibility. I could never understand why she felt she had a place or say when it came to *my* daughter. But the truth is he lies to get his way. Of course, she believed everything he told her.

I never truly felt like Paul valued a woman like me. The truth is, I don't think he was ever really into me at all. I don't think he wanted to be with someone who is smart, outspoken, and independent. He needed someone he could control. I think that his issues with his mother took a toll on him psychologically. I don't believe Paul likes women in general. He plays games, he's abusive in every way possible, and he's rude. He wants someone to be with him for the sake of his ego and his need to control a woman the way his mother controlled him is just who he is. He's not looking for someone to love and build a life with. He needs someone to take his anger out on. I felt bad for Paul. I *really* tried to be there for him. I tried to show him the support he never had. But he rejected me every chance he got. When I was with Paul, I always felt like I was doing something wrong. I allowed the abuse to put me in a depressive state. Even my family noticed that I wasn't the bubbly person I once was. He's a textbook narcissist; unable to hold himself accountable and manipulative. I couldn't be vulnerable with him. If I cried in front of him, he had something negative to say about that which made me vow to **never** show my true feelings in front of him. Over time, I gradually fell out of love with him. I am not male-bashing, I am just sharing my experience so you can avoid the pain I've endured.

His issues were bleeding into my daughter's life. He did his best to keep a wedge between me and my daughter. He wanted her to believe that I just up and left her with no explanation and that just wasn't the case. He knows that. But it's all a part of his plan to punish me and control her. When I attend family functions and I want her to go with me, he does *everything* he can to stop it. Paul is emotionally abusive to my daughter as well. When she's upset with him, he ignores her and won't speak to her. He tells her what she can and can't eat. He wants to control everything with her and refuses to compromise. He treats her the same way he was treating me. So I enrolled her in counseling. She knows both her parents work hard and love her. But she's afraid of him and she shouldn't have to be.

Now that my daughter is a little older, she expressed her true feelings about her father to me. Apparently he speaks negatively about me in front of her. Of course, she doesn't like that. It's difficult to have to watch her endure that pain and not be able to stand up for me. He has his opinions of me and that's fine. Sometimes, no matter what you do it won't be received well by others. That's a reflection of the unresolved issues they have with themselves. Don't allow it to stop you. The bond I have with my daughter is so much better now because she and I are talking a lot more. I'm doing my best to show her what a strong woman looks like in hopes that she'll gain strength and her voice from me demonstrating that same behavior.

Paul's vindictive nature knows no bounds. I received a call from my daughter's school one day, they asked me to come to the school. It wasn't an urgent matter concerning my daughter but she did ask them to call me instead of her father. When I arrived they advised me that he'd given them a written note stating, I wasn't allowed to take my daughter from the school campus. My new attorney went over the contract that I signed with my old lawyer and he gave me a thorough breakdown of what I signed exactly. He was furious that my last lawyer dropped the ball and advised me to sign a contract that was so one-sided. He informed me that I did indeed sign away my parental rights. So now, we're back to the original agreement of him having her during the week and I get her on the weekends. We're still currently going to court for custody of my daughter. I filed for 50/50 custody of her. He managed to avoid getting served and filed right behind me. But he filed for sole custody with no visitation. I was attempting to be fair but since that's the game he wanted to play, I changed my filing to sole custody as well.

I didn't date anyone for 2 years after I left Paul. I had a really good friend,

Daryl, who became closer over the time he and I were spending together. In the beginning, it was difficult to figure out if we were dating or not because we'd been friends for so long. When we had a discussion about us, I told him that I felt like we should wait one year before we decide to be in a relationship. He was floored with the timeframe I suggested. He said, "don't you want a baby by then?" Daryl was a great guy and we dated for *several* years. During our relationship, he fell ill and was diagnosed with a sickness that was incurable. He said he didn't want me to have to deal with this for the rest of my life so we went our separate ways.

In the past, I used my eyes to determine the men I would entertain. Now I look at a man with my ears. I listen now. I'm a lot more selective with who I give my phone number to and what position I want to give them in my life if any. How a man treats me is a non-negotiable dealbreaker. Not that a man has to kiss my ass, but I do expect a certain level of respect and I want to be treated as a lady should. Now, I refuse to compromise how I want to be treated and respected. I had to figure out what exactly I wanted from a man. I know I want a protector and a provider. Which brings me to the question, *what does that kind of man want from me?*

As we define or redefine our dating core values, be mindful that our emotions drive our decisions, especially in romantic relationships. Oftentimes, those emotions can lead us to decisions we regret or make decisions that only benefit the other person. For so long, I didn't think that men had feelings because many of them tend to hide them so well. I've learned it's important to be just as gentle with them as we want them to be with us. I learned a lot about men in my last relationship. I also learned a lot about how to be a lady and what attracts a man. Let the man *be* a man; sit back and be feminine. Don't lean forward to do anything he's supposed to do. Doing *his* job doesn't prove your independence, it shows your masculine energy and makes him feel like he's up against another man. Your power is in your femininity. Let go of control and allow yourself to be cherished. Men will step up when you step down. You can be an alpha female, just hang your balls up when you get home. Men want to be your hero. They want to feel needed for all the manly duties that may need to be done in your life. Lean on him and know that it's okay to do so. That doesn't make you weak. It may take some time but the natural balance of the masculine and feminine will take place. If you want to understand how to attract a man and stay in your feminine energy:

1. **Stop being careless about how you look.** Men are visual creatures. Present your best self at all times. You don't have to show it all to get attention. Leave a lot to the imagination.
2. **Stop accepting everything.** Don't always give the benefit of the doubt. Put yourself on a pedestal. It may be difficult because it's not natural but it's necessary to receive the treatment you deserve. Men will only go as far as you allow them to. Don't let him off the hook when he gives excuses.
3. **Stop pursuing men.** If you want to be the feminine energy in the relationship, stop your pursuit. Men are simple. Boost their ego and get what you want.

Whether you're single and dating or not dating at all, it's important to work on yourself. Get comfortable with evolving. Your life won't be complete because you added someone to it. You have to already be complete when the right one shows up in your life. As you date, be alert when a guy behaves as if he's just not that into you. You have to come to the table knowing who you are and what you want. If he acts as if he doesn't want you, then he is not the one for you. Don't get caught up in the hype of being in a relationship without having done the necessary self-work. If you do, when the dust settles, you'll still be lost. Finding yourself doesn't come from a man, a relationship, or a marriage. Only you can define you. Otherwise, you'll be setting yourself up for failure. **The only way a man will value, respect, and adore you is if you first feel that way about yourself.**

"Women need to hear other women talk about the things we're embarrassed to talk about. I refuse to be hurt again. I WILL be treated like a queen and I am treating myself like a queen FIRST!"

~TAINA ANTHONY

Patterns

By: Taina Anthony

*W*omen are good at hiding. We hide behind our smiles, our success, our relationships, and our materialistic gain. We work so hard on looking like we're together when the truth is, inside, most of us are a mess. A mess because of our past. A mess with men. A mess as a result of our pain. But we don't tell anyone that. We put on the armor so no one notices. We put on a mask as a way to convince ourselves and others that things are exactly as they appear…great; when that couldn't be any further from the truth. We need to start being **real** with ourselves and each other. But how? How can we be honest when we're ashamed? How can we be honest when our pain is a secret we're not willing to tell? Women need to hear other women being truthful about their pain and past experiences. We have a tendency to hide out of shame or embarrassment. Had I known better; had I heard other women discussing the truth about themselves and their pasts, I probably wouldn't have suffered so much. But I didn't have anyone around me that was interested in sharing their truth. I truly believe someone else's story of triumph would've saved me a lot of heartache. I've been in multiple relationships and long ones at that. I'd always left one relationship and jumped into another so every guy I was with was a rebound from the previous one. I was in a vicious cycle of dysfunction and the pattern of pain continued until I stopped the cycle.

January 1994 was when I got into a relationship with my first boyfriend, Jermaine. He and I were together from 12 years old until we graduated high school in August of 1999. We broke up because he cheated on me more than once. I forgave him the first two times, but when the girl he cheated on me with revealed her pregnancy, I was done. I couldn't forgive that. He was my high school sweetheart and had he not impregnated another girl, I would've stayed with him. Our relationship was beautiful, but Jermaine taught me that men are going to be men and they'll change when they're ready.

It was September 1999 and I was 18 years old. That's when I met Terry, my daughter's (**2 daughters)** father. We met one day while I was outside walking. I kept running into him but we never really met. This time he pulled his car over and asked me to take his number. I resisted but he stood there reciting his phone number over and over again, so many times that I actually remembered it. When I met up with my best friend, I told her about him and she insisted that I give him a chance. But her reasoning for pushing me towards him was only to help me get over Jermaine. She lived by the motto, "to get over one person, you have to get under a new one." It's not always the best idea to listen to other people. I wasn't sure I should, but I called him anyway. We went on a double date and our relationship began from there. We had fun but he had a serious jealousy streak. If he thought I was looking at another man he assumed I wanted that man. He'd get verbally abusive and lash out. When we were in public, he didn't want me to look at or speak to anyone. My relationship with him didn't feel right but I was young and went along with it. After he was verbally abusive, he'd apologize saying he couldn't control his emotions. The apology was definitely no consolation for his behavior. But he continued behaving in the same manner and I kept forgiving him for it. So what incentive did he have to change?

One night, we were on a double date with my best friend and his brother at Red Lobster. We were eating and talking, having a good time. I looked up at his brother and he got upset about that, whispering in my ear, asking me if I wanted to have sex with his brother. His jealousy and need to control me was ridiculous. I was furious about his comment. So much so that I spoke up and out loud. He wanted to whisper but I'd had it with him. Loudly, I told him that I wasn't interested in his brother. He was so embarrassed that he took the noodles and threw them in my face. I got up from the table and walked away. I was embarrassed. I started crying when I was out of his eyesight. I knew I had to leave him and I told him I was done. The night only worsened from there. When he found me crying, he started calling me names and threatening that I'd better not leave. He choked me that night and threatened to kill me and our daughter if I left him. Apparently his aunt was there having dinner as well and noticed he and I. She walked over to us and instantly began praying for him. He broke down and started crying, telling me he didn't know what was wrong with him, blah, blah blah. He always used that tactic as a way to manipulate me into forgiving him. That same night, I left with my best friend. This is just one of many incidents that happened this way.

Interestingly, he didn't just abuse me. He also abused my best friend. He'd get jealous when I hung out with my girlfriends so he'd called them bitches and hoes. They'd get upset with him and argue back with him. So everything went from, "you should call him" to "you need to get away from him." I only had one friend that gave me a truth that was hard to ignore. She told me that she would never tell me to leave him, that I'd leave him when I had enough. I never forgot her words. She was right. I left him when I was done being abused.

Once, Terry punched me in the head after I'd given birth to our second daughter. I knew I had to get away from him for good. I called my Dad and told him everything that had been going on. Usually, I kept these episodes to myself. When my father came over, he asked me what I wanted to do. I told him that I wanted Terry to leave. Terry was living with me in my house at the time. My Dad spoke to him and made him leave. In less than 30 days, I'd found another place and moved. 30 days before I left, my Dad changed the locks on the door; some nights I felt safer spending the night at my Dad's.

Every time Terry got abusive, he'd apologize saying, "I'm sorry,'" but his actions never matched those words. I attempted to leave Terry on several occasions. But he cried every time I tried to leave and each time I stayed because I felt sorry for him. I thought that I could fix men and that was my biggest problem. I thought if I stayed, he would be different. I thought my patience would fix them.

I'm a daddy's girl and always have been. I didn't lack male attention and love because I'd gotten it from my father all my life. However, my father was abusive toward me. If I stepped out of line or was disrespectful to my mother, he would beat me with a belt. Each time it happened, he'd feel so bad for beating me that he'd come to me apologizing and professing his love. And I forgave him every time. It's no wonder, my relationship with Terry had the same dynamic.

Terry and I broke up indefinitely, in May of 2006. All along, I had a friend named Chance. I began hanging out with Chance in July 2006. He was a model and extremely good looking. He'd always been just a friend and I did find him attractive but he was boring because he was shy. He didn't seem to have much personality and while I was physically attracted to him, that's all it was. We hung out a lot. But I was one that made everything we did interesting. He was more monotone and I didn't have much conversation to give. I knew it wasn't going to work out. I was talking to another guy at the same time who was a little more lively. In September 2006, I decided to move on from Chance because moving forward with him wasn't an option. I was wasting my time hanging out with him and figured that out relatively quickly.

In June 2006, I met someone to fill the voids, Brandon. I believe I was more open and trusting with Brandon because we had a lot of mutual friends. We went to the same high school and although we didn't know one another personally, we knew of one another. We met via MySpace, which was a social media outlet prior to the introduction of Facebook, etc. One day he 'liked' one of my pictures and that's how everything began. We talked a lot. The conversation was feeding my soul because, at the time, I felt empty and lonely. He was the first person to talk to me and give me attention so I went for it. We decided to meet up in person. He was kind of heavy with big lips. If I'm being honest, I wasn't attracted to him. But I ignored that feeling. I told myself to be open. We began hanging out, going to clubs and drinking. I was in my early 20's and hadn't experienced this side of adulthood quite yet, so I was enjoying myself. This routine became a weekly thing. We were partying and drinking. Interestingly, we didn't have sex for about 10 months. I kept telling him I wasn't ready to have sex with him but the truth is, I simply wasn't attracted to him in that way. I felt like the lack of sex was what allowed us to actually connect. I fell in love with who he was as a person. We grew into a more serious relationship. About 10 months into the relationship, I allowed him to meet my children.

When I was comfortable enough and we were in a committed relationship, I allowed him to spend the night. Sometimes Terry would show up acting crazy. He would do things like sit in front of my house just to see if there was another man coming or going. One night my daughter's father came to my house and pulled up beside me and Brandon. He brandished a gun at us and I asked Brandon not to get out of the car. He was not happy about being threatened and like any man, he wasn't letting it fly. But he listened to me and stayed in the car. When Terry finally drove off, we did the same. But he was laying low somewhere because he followed up for a few blocks. Oddly, Terry never came back around after that. After the incident, I told Brandon I didn't think the relationship was going to work. I told him that I didn't want him to get hurt and I wasn't 100% sure Terry wouldn't take his threat a step further. I didn't know what he was capable of. But Brandon had a different idea. He told me that he was in love with me and wanted to move forward.

I felt like I settled for Brandon. I was in my 20's when that relationship began. Over the years following our initial commitment to one another, I started to evolve. I was beginning to want more out of my own life. I've always been a goal-driven person. The problem was, Brandon wasn't. He was lazy. I was active. He wasn't. I was starting to see that the only relation in this relationship was drinking and partying. But I was over partying. I knew that...and I still stayed, *settling*. When he asked me to marry him, I was more sold out to the idea of getting married rather than *who* I was marrying.

I knew I had doubts but I still went through with it. Everyone told us they thought we were a cute couple. I got caught up in the fantasy and we never grew from that. As time moved forward, I was no longer able to keep up the lie. I asked myself, *how do I get out of this relationship?* Deep down, I knew he wasn't who I wanted to be with. I allowed myself to believe that I should stay because we had children. Oftentimes, you can be in the same, house, same bed, but not the same relationship. I was a single, married woman if that makes sense.

Yes, we could have gotten marriage counseling. In fact, at one point, I suggested that we go. He didn't want to go because he didn't "want people in our business." The truth is, most people are afraid of the vulnerability and the exposure that counseling brings. He asked me why I wanted to attend counseling and I attempted to have an honest conversation with him but nothing ever got resolved.

The years continued and so did my unhappiness. When I reached my threshold of unhappiness, I told him that I couldn't move forward with him anymore; that I wasn't happy and I wanted to separate. When he knew that I was serious, he suggested we go to marriage counseling. I was past that stage. I asked him to go to marriage counseling 4 years prior and he wasn't interested. By this time, we hadn't been having sex for several months on end. That caused a lot of problems as well.

Over the course of my marriage, things changed, and not for the better. I was doing well with my multi-level marketing business. I was traveling at the expense of the company and attending seminars all over the country. I'd always invited Brandon to attend the trips with me but he usually declined. Again, in my eyes he was lazy. All he wanted to do was play video games, drink with his friends, gamble, and just be at home with the kids. He didn't want to better himself and that created a lot of distance between us. It felt like Brandon didn't want to be a part of what I was doing. As I got deeper into the MLM business, I met a lot of like-minds.

A lot of my sideline multi-level marketing team are very fit and good looking...especially the men. And they flirted all the time. But I honored my marriage and declined offers to cheat left and right. But there was this one man, *James*. He was a distributor for the company as well. He became one of my mentor's and we spent a lot of time working together. We were both married and knew it was better that we didn't cross that line, but we did. When the company hosted seminars, we'd be in the same place. Our affair began in October 2016. He invited me to his room to look over some numbers and one thing led to another. James and I had a relationship for almost 3 years and I was very tight-lipped about it. We tried filling in the void that was missing from our marriages. I told him that I was going to divorce Brandon. But he had no intention of divorcing his wife. Sometimes she'd attend the seminars and I wasn't sure if he thought I was supposed to put up with him ignoring me when she was in attendance. This was not right. We almost got caught by his wife because of an extra friendly hug. I had to ask myself, *girl, what are you doing?* I had to be honest, I knew what I was doing wasn't right. Here I was going to church and doing things I had no business doing. There was no need in denying it. I never set out to cheat on my husband or ruin anyone else's marriage. It happened out of the lack in my own marriage and unhappiness in my own life.

I've been in several abusive relationships. The pain I endured from each relationship stayed with me long after it was over. I carried the wounds from the abuse and I projected that pain onto each new man I came in contact with thereafter. But it wasn't just the men I'd been romantically involved with that contributed to my lack of sense of self. The abuse began when I was a little girl.

In Hispanic families, they made a difference between Latinos that were fair-skinned and dark-skinned. If you were fair-skinned, you were superior to those that were dark-skinned. My parents are both Latino but my father was dark-skinned and my mother's family had a problem with that. I grew up in the contents of racism within my own family. They called me the N-word in Spanish a lot. I wasn't accepted by my family and it caused me to hate the skin that I was in. My mother and I had a very difficult relationship. She never accepted who I was. I thought she didn't love me. I always felt like she was embarrassed of me because I was dark-skinned. Sometimes when we were in public and people would ask her if I was her daughter, she'd say no and tell them that I was adopted or that she was babysitting me.

I was also sexually abused by my mother. One night, she walked in the house drunk and began touching me and trying to take my clothes off. My father walked in and pulled her off me and dragged her out. I don't know what happened after that. I remember crying myself to sleep and erasing that incident from my mind. I never addressed that event with her. But she wasn't the only one that was sexually abusive towards me. My maternal grandfather always wanted me to sit on his lap so he could put his hand up my dress. My male cousins on my mother's side also sexually abused me. I'd always felt embarrassed about the abuse so I never talked about it. I was a little black girl who didn't speak English and all I really wanted was to be accepted.

I'd also witnessed my father's abuse toward my mother. Sometimes she had a black eye or welts on her body due to being hit with a belt. My mother also drank a lot. As my siblings and I got older, the abuse happened less. However, it had lasting effects.

Due to the affair and the long years of unhappiness, I knew things had to change. I couldn't keep this charade up. Brandon was shocked when I asked for a divorce. It was as if he didn't see anything wrong with our marriage. I told him that we could no longer live together and he needed to leave. He moved out and went to his mother's in March 2019. But I don't think he believed I was serious until I served him the divorce papers. When he received the documents, he texted me and asked me if I was sure I wanted to move forward with the divorce. I hadn't been more sure of anything in my life. He told me that he was hurt but he knew he wasn't the man that I wanted. He said he knew that I wanted a life that was contradictory to what he was willing to provide. He was okay with just taking care of his family. He was okay with a 9 to 5 job. According to the life I want to live, this was settling and after reflecting on this relationship from start to finish, I learned that I couldn't do that to myself. I thought I should stay because we had children together. The divorce took a while because I was the one stalling. I had family members and friends that had their own opinions, mainly opinions that suggested we could work things out. I was being told that because we had children together, we needed to stay together. But no one knows your relationship the way you do. No one knows what really goes on behind the closed door. We'd been going through a rough patch that lasted 3 years. I was miserable and couldn't take it anymore. Suffering through a 14-year marriage full of unhappiness wasn't what was best for me or my children. I learned that it was okay to put myself first. So I chose happiness. The divorce was peaceful and we didn't fight through it. That's how I knew, *it was time.* I had to be strong enough to ask myself, *what do you want?*

I was still having the affair throughout my divorce. But that was no longer making me happy either. I cried a lot when I was having this affair. The guilt was eating at me. Every time I attempted to end things with us, we just ended right back together. I was running then end up right back with him. I told him that I knew he wasn't going to leave his wife although I was leaving Brandon. He tried to convince me that I shouldn't leave Brandon and even offered to counsel us. Something had to be wrong with him. The odd thing was, James didn't want me to leave him alone either. Basically, he was saying he wanted to have his cake and eat it too. No! In August 2019 I cut all ties. I couldn't be second to anyone. I had to choose me in spite of the men that didn't see my value. My divorce that was finalized as of April 2020. This was me, choosing me.

No one ever sat me down and talked to me about men per se; what to do and what not to do. My father was like most men. He cared about money and felt like I should be with a man that wasn't lacking financially. He felt like a man that was broken physically was also broke mentally and vice versa with a man who was financially comfortable. On the other hand, my mother taught me how to be the woman of the house. (ie, cook, clean, iron clothes etc.) She always had me help her keep the house up so I'm strong in that area. One day I came home with a hickey on my neck and my mother noticed it. She didn't chastise me or out me to my father (who would have flipped out if he'd seen it), but she used that moment as an opportunity to teach me different. She told me that I should have more respect for myself and not to allow anyone to put marks like that on my body. That was the last time I let a man put a hickey on me. It was a powerful lesson. It was a part of teaching me how to be a lady. I knew then, that I needed to be more discreet about what I was doing. But none of that taught me how to choose a man or how to deal with the ups and downs of a relationship. I had to find a way to do that on my own. That said, it was time for me to deal with me.

I began seeing a life coach a few years ago. During one session the life coach walked everyone through a meditation. The coach wanted us to dig up our deep-seated issues. All of the abuse came up as I was meditating. It never occurred to me that I didn't know my worth and my childhood was the reason why I accepted men that weren't worth my time. The sexual abuse moment with my mother also came up and all I could do was cry. I knew then that I needed to deal with that wound. When the life coach asked for a volunteer, I raised my hand. I told everyone in the room about what happened between my mother and I. The coach asked me to imagine my mother was in the room and he asked me to talk to her; tell her what was on my heart. I did and I released the pain at that moment. While she wasn't actually in the room to hear what I had to say, I felt like I talked to her about it. I was no longer in bondage and made peace with it.

Right after Brandon and I broke up, I fell back into the same pattern of looking for acceptance in a man. I needed a rebound and it was no surprise that I found one, Aaron. He was a friend of one of Brandon's friends. He wasn't initially upfront about his interest in me. I'm a distributor for a multi level marketing organization, which is a fitness and health regimen. He approached me about signing up for the program. He and I began a friendship from there. I was assisting him on his journey to lose weight. The attraction was there instantly and apparently he was feeling the same way because he began flirting. I'd laugh and brush it off. But it got more aggressive as we continued working with each other. At the time I was running my business out of a place I was leasing. One day we were in my office and he grabbed me and kissed me. We started hanging out on a more personal level. We did a lot of outside activities which I liked. We became intimate and I was enjoying him. I began feeling like I loved him. He gave me passion and intimacy; something I'd never experienced before.

One thing I noticed is I was falling in the trap of someone that had the same nature and tendencies as Terry. He had a bad habit of throwing other women in my face. He'd make rude comments or share information with me about other women he was dealing with. One incident occurred after we were intimate and it was time for me to leave. He implied that he was interested in another woman who was financially well off. Granted, he and I weren't in any committed relationship. But I still didn't understand his need to do that. There was an incident when he invited me over and didn't answer the door even though his car was there. He then accused me of stalking him and being crazy. I didn't see it then and I thought I was in love with him but I was really tied to him because the sex was so intimate and passionate. I couldn't leave him alone. I kept going back to him. I guess I felt like he gave me something that I wouldn't find elsewhere. It was like he studied me. He told me that he waited years to talk to me because of my relationship with Brandon. I enjoyed the thought of being the object of someone's desire. He seemed perfect. But he was downright mean and mentally abusive and I couldn't subject myself to him any longer. Aaron had a lot of internal issues he needed to resolve without me around.

I'd always participated in dysfunctional relationships out of my need for acceptance and lack of self-respect. Now I'm divorced with 4 children and I know who I am. My back is straighter, I hold my head higher, and I accept myself. In the past, I was dishonoring myself throughout all of my relationships. When I do start dating, it will be different because I'm different. I'm currently single and plan on staying that way until I'm whole. Once I can say, beyond a doubt, that I know my worth, I'm confident, and I know what I want, then I will consider opening myself up to dating. But everything starts with you. If your heart and mind isn't right, then it won't matter how you look on the outside.

I'm in the process of reinventing myself. I'm learning how to walk away from anything that isn't serving me. I encourage women to do the same. Don't settle and don't ignore the red flags. Not only the red flags you detect in a man, but the red flags you also detect in yourself. Oftentimes, women will determine that we can put up with poor behavior from a man because we're interested in them. Don't be so desperate that you turn a blind eye to what is so clearly, unacceptable behavior. Honor your own boundaries. That's the only way someone else will do the same. I'm still in the process of clearing the debris and learning what it means to date with intention. I'm discovering **me**. I'm discovering what kind of characteristics I desire in a mate. I want to manifest the right man. I made a list of characteristics that I desire in the man I truly wanted to give myself to.

I want a man that is:

- Respectful and a Gentleman
- Goal Oriented
- Visionary and ambitious
- Handyman
- Loves to spoil his woman and enjoys it
- Keeps his woman's car nice and clean
- Educated
- Loves elevated business conversations
- Dresses to impress all the time
- Keeps himself well-groomed
- Works smart
- Earns Over 200,000 a year minimum
- Enjoys working out
- Enjoys socializing with everyone
- Great Energy
- 6 feet tall or above
- Caramel color complexion
- Greet teeth and smile
- Outgoing
- Loves to travel and be spontaneous
- Freaky and nasty (sexually)
- Faithful to our relationship
- Business-minded
- Supports his woman in what she loves to do
- Enjoys working out with a group of people
- Loves kids
- Allows his woman to handle her business

- Confident
- Homeowner or goals to purchase a home
- Strong and Sexy
- Gentle with his words
- Caring
- Loveable
- Always makes sure his woman is financially well
- Has a little roughness in him
- Cooks from time to time
- Open to learning and do Herbalife business with me
- Be able to lead me in the right direction
- Believes in God
- Speaks my love language

When I do start dating again, I plan to have open and honest communication with a man. I won't be embarrassed or scared to ask the questions I need answers to so that I'm not wasting my time or his. I want to truly know what I'm getting myself into. I want to know that person from the inside. When I start dating, I'll be dating with the intention of being in a committed relationship. I want to make sure that my potential mate has goals and aspirations that are in alignment with mine.

I do have to be physically attracted to a man. For me, that is important. However, moving forward, I won't allow that to be the driving force behind the reason I choose someone and continue choosing them. I plan to get to know him by listening and allowing them to share their experiences with me. I want to be treated like a queen and I plan to be with someone who will treat me that way. I want the person I manifested based on my list of needs, not the one I settled for.

It is possible to press the reset button, but you must begin your journey to true love **starting with you.** You won't be able to recognize, let alone, enjoy the fruits of *real love* until you learn how to love yourself. I'm still on my journey of self-discovery and nothing is going to stand in the way of that. I want to be ready when God gives me the man I deserve.

"Make sure you become the type of person you'd want your son or daughter to bring home to you."

~ INA MEKESHA

I Will Not Compromise!

By: Ina Mekesha

*M*y brother and I grew up in a southern, two-parent home where certain topics were never discussed. As the years went by, my brother noticed the physical differences between him and my dad. He knew they were polar opposites and began to question paternity. My brother was over six-feet-tall, my father was a relatively short man, and so was my mother. He had good reason to wonder if he was truly my father's son. When we were teenagers, my parents disclosed the truth. My father was not my brother's father, but my brother and father are extremely close and have a super father-son bond. It takes a stand out guy to take the responsibility of another man's child. No matter what this is POPS. My brother was relieved by the news. Unfortunately, my brother didn't have a relationship with his biological father until he became an adult. My father thought of himself as a "ladies man". As a result, I have a sister that is the same age as me. We've always known about our sister. She was never a secret.

My father loved to party just like me. It wasn't unusual for him to come home in the wee hours of the morning. He was a good, mild-mannered, and understanding man, however, he never showed me what I should be looking for in a man. We never talked about relationships or how a man was supposed to treat me. My mom would throw out vague comments like, *"make sure you get someone who is going to take care of you."* **But what does that mean?** She'd always throw out random statements but never expounded on the rules of love, sex, or relationships. Unfortunately, I did not grow up in an environment where I could be open about my feelings towards the opposite sex. Whatever my parents said was how things went. I didn't feel comfortable with asking questions about sex. If I did, I knew the response would be something like, "Why are you asking about that? Don't have sex until you're married!"

My mother took care of everything in the house. My mother was the sweetest woman you could meet, but she wasn't to be played with. She has a very strong, old school tough personality. Her intimidating personality prevented me from doing things that were important to me. I probably would've made better choices in men if I was able to present them to her without being judged. She was a 'because-I-said-so' kind of woman. I was never able to verbally express myself because she didn't respect my opinion due to her tough personality.

I met my oldest son's father, David, at Rancho High School in 1990. He was tall and dark, just like I liked it. We lived around the corner from one another, and although I found him attractive, I was shy and never pursued anything with him. We met our freshman year, lost touch in our sophomore year because I transferred to another school. Then we reconnected during our junior year of high school. We were just friends until I graduated. I don't remember how or when I gave him my phone number, but we started talking more and going out to dinner. Our relationship formed from there. I dated him throughout my twenties. Marriage was never a topic of conversation. We were young, having fun, and enjoying one another's company.

One night we were hanging out. One thing led to another, and we had sex. I knew we had conceived at that very moment. We'd been intimate before; however, something felt different about that time. I told him that I knew I was pregnant, and he quickly denied my intuition. He thought I was just emotional. Of course, I wasn't able to prove it that night, but *I just knew*. I waited a few weeks to see if I'd miss my cycle, and I did. I went to the doctor for confirmation, and just as I expected, I was pregnant. When I told him I was pregnant, he did not react. I thought he'd be excited, but his response was indifferent. We told his family about the pregnancy, and they were fine with it.

On the other hand, I hid my pregnancy from my family. My family has a strong religious background, and I thought I'd get kicked out if I told them. Most importantly, I didn't want to disappoint them. My family taught us that you're not supposed to have sex until you are married. **No exceptions.** I clearly struggled with this "rule". I explored dating, sex, and relationships on my own. I learned more tough lessons that I probably needed to. If I'd just understood my worth, could I have made better choices?

After my son was born in 1999, I found out that my boyfriend was keeping up with an old female friend from high school. I didn't think anything of it because I believe that men and women can have a strictly platonic relationship. I came to find out that she was not the platonic friend he painted her to be. Our relationship suffered after the birth of our son. I noticed how the responsibility of being a parent and meeting the needs of our newborn son overwhelmed him. Things became worse when I went back to work. I had secured a good job working for the public school district. We placed our son in daycare; however, my son's father couldn't hold up his end of the financial bargain, and my frustration was **building**. When I explained how his lack of financial support for our son affected me, he immediately pulled away from the relationship. He neglected me emotionally and both of us financially he was always present for our son physically. We were arguing about finances and his immature behavior almost daily, which eventually ripped our relationship apart. I decided it was time for us to take a break. He decided to go to his mother's house until we could figure out how we would move forward.

One day, I went to his mother's house to drop my son off to his father. When I arrived, I noticed there was someone sitting outside in a chair. When she saw me, she immediately put her head down. I didn't pay it too much attention because my hands were so full. I thought she might have been related to him. On the way out the house, David started following me to my car. As he was following me, I saw the girl stand up. I took a good look at her and I knew who she was; the "friend" from high school. When I called her name, she looked at me with the most disgusted look, then rolled her eyes. I looked at him and thought, *really? Out of ALL the girls you could have cheated on me with, you chose Sandra?* At that moment, I had a clear understanding of what was going on. I didn't say one word. I refused to give either of them any energy. I got in my car and went out with my friends. At this point, he had to come clean about his "friendship" with Sandra. She hated my guts because she felt like (she should have been the first to have his child. Having a child was definitely not something that I was in competition with anyone. She was telling him a whole bunch of nonsense and he was feeding into it! A week later, he officially moved in with her. I was done with him but I never kept my son from him or his family after we broke up.

One night in 2000, while we were at the club, my cousin noticed that a tall light-skinned man was staring at me. I looked back at him and she was urging me to go dance with him. I kept refusing. As we were moving around the club, we bumped into him and she spoke up. "Hey! This is my cousin, Ina. I saw you looking at her. You wanna dance?" He said yes and we danced to *Shake it Fast by Mystical*. His name was Xavier who had great conversation and was a pretty good dancer. We talked, exchanged numbers, and the next day, met up for lunch.

It took about a month before Xavier and I became intimate. Mentally, I was in a space of needing to feel wanted by someone and I filled that void with sex. He and I weren't in an exclusive relationship, we were in a *situationship*. He'd take me to his parents house because he still had a room there. One day while we were there, a woman showed up. Not just any woman, **she was his girlfriend**. I don't believe she knew about me and I certainly didn't know about her. I wasn't one who indulged in confrontation and I had no position with him to protect, so I left. I wasn't so into him that I wanted to put up a fight. Physically and sexually, I was attracted to him but nothing beyond that. Of course, he called and lied. He said she was his ex-girlfriend. It didn't matter because after that, I left him alone.

A few days later, I went to my favorite spot, *Club Zaza*. I decided to buy myself a shot and noticed a short woman standing on the staircase nearby. She didn't even look like she belonged in the club. I didn't pay her any mind until she approached me with a heavy accent, "*Hey, you shouldn't drink when you're pregnant.*" I was shocked at what she was saying. I thought, who is this lady? And who is pregnant? I took the shot and continued my night. One week went by and I was still stuck on the lady in the club. The spooky thing is, my cycle was actually late. I kept a menstrual cycle tracker on my phone and I'd mark my cycle on my calendar. Was the lady from the club right after all? I wasn't dealing with Xavier after running into his girlfriend and there was no way I was dealing with David. Once I went to the doctor and took a pregnancy test that confirmed I was indeed pregnant. I knew I had to call him and let him know. He didn't have much of a reaction when I told him. He asked me what I'd planned to do. I told him that I was going to keep the baby. He didn't care whether I had the baby or not. Once again, I was on my own.

David and Sandra eventually had a daughter together. So we both had one child outside of one another. Even though things were complicated between

David and me, he accepted the role as a father to my second son and I was happy about that. I'd always wanted a traditional family. In the eyes of society, black women are always single mothers, and I had no desire to be another statistic. My brother gave me some advice that I didn't agree with. Basically, he said that I may as well marry my oldest son's father because most men will not want to raise another man's child. The truth is, I'd rather my children have no father-figure in their lives than for them to have a bad example. That led me to feel like I should try to make things work with him. He'd already broken things off with Sandra so he decided to come back home.

David and I decided to get married. Trying to make things work was very difficult for me. His immaturity towards real responsibility made it hard to deal with him. In turn, it made it hard to stay with. He refused to pull his weight financially and he still wanted to act as if we were in High School! I found myself nagging and complaining all the time about his lack of support. We were supposed to be partners, but I never knew what that felt like. Our sons felt the tension and heard the arguments all the time. We were even staying in separate rooms. One day I came home from work and my sons told me that David moved his things out of the house while I was gone. Apparently, he was having conversations with the boys about me behind my back which is why they weren't surprised that he was leaving. They told me he even took my recipe book. My recipe book? Talk about immature. I didn't even call him once I knew he was gone. If he wanted me to know where he was, he would've had a conversation with me. My boys and I headed to Home Depot to buy the things needed to change the locks. David was no longer welcomed in our home.

Later on that night, David called the boys and expressed his irritation that I hadn't called him after he'd left. I refused to allow him to get under my skin or interrupt the boys' peace. He tried to come back to the house while I was gone and was furious he couldn't get in. He told the boys that he forgot something. He didn't forget anything. He was just upset and confused by my reaction to his departure. He was a coward for doing things like that and I didn't owe him anything. I'd had enough of taking care of a man who refused to do his part. I was no longer going to neglect my wants, feelings, and desires. I decided to move on just like he did and I never looked back.

When I reflect on the choices I've made, I wish I'd followed my dreams.

When I graduated high school, I wanted to go to Grambling State but my mother told me no. I knew my grades weren't where they should've been but her stance discouraged me from college all together. Even though I'd secured a well-paying job at the public school district, and in a relationship with my son's father, I was still a single mother. I held all the responsibility. I attempted to go back to school but had to put my education on hold because I didn't have the support I needed from David to continue. But by the time my second son was born, **I wanted more**. I decided to go back to school but I wasn't able to finish because I had so much responsibility being a parent.

If you are in a similar situation or contemplating staying in a less than fulfilling relationship, consider the following before doing so:

1. **Take care of yourself!** Put yourself first. Even though we are single parents, putting ourselves first is top priority. We cannot pour from an empty cup.
2. **Accomplish your goals!** Give yourself timelines and dates. Always tend to your own dreams. Don't lose sight of them no matter what!
3. **Budget your finances!** Set yourself up so that you're not looking for a man for financial security.
4. **Don't Waste Your Time!** Ask the guy you are dating, "Are you the type of guy you'd want your daughter to bring home?" If he stutters or cannot give you an answer, RUN for your life!

Dating can be difficult as a single mother. I know we all want love and there's no need to hide that. However, try building a true friendship with someone first. You'll know you're with the right person when you don't need to have sex and still want to be in their presence. There are key indicators a woman should look for when dating: *Can you be yourself with this person? Can you truly laugh with them? Can you two talk about anything? Can you be honest with one another?* If all you have is sex, you're wasting your time.

I learned a lot about myself and my needs as I went back and forth with my ex. I knew I wanted more and deserved more. Even though my sons are adults, I've learned to always consider my needs and date people who are in alignment with my core values and life goals. Single Moms, don't make any decisions about a relationship without considering your children. I am not saying you have to wait until they are adults to date, however, you only have 18 precious years to give them a firm foundation for them to become productive citizens who thrive in relationships.

When my ex left, I saw that as my chance to start over. It's okay to start over and be open to a relationship full of friendship, partnership, *and* love. **I will not compromise** and neither should you! It is crucial for you to know what you deserve and never settle. Love yourself, crush your goals, and be open to living the life YOU want without regret.

"Walk away from the men who don't deserve your attention so that you're not exhausted when the right one comes along."

~ SHI CIRON

No More Talking!

By: Shi Ciron

I grew up in the church. I'd known the pastor and first lady of my church since I was a baby; we're practically family. With that being said, I was one of many children that the elders kept an eye on. I also grew up knowing the pastors children very well. As we got older, the pastor made a joke that I should date his youngest son, Amir. I didn't think much of it but over time, he and I became friends. We went out on a couple of dates which meant, we were 'going out.' That was the term we used for a boyfriend/girlfriend situation at that time.

Amir and I started talking in 2007 then we took a break because I found out he was also talking to another female. We were friends on social media and I'd often tag him in my posts. One day I posted that I was going to see my boo and out of nowhere, I'd gotten a message in my DM saying that he was seeing some other chick. I thought to myself, *'thanks for the information.'* I brought that up to him and of course, he denied it. I wasn't buying it. So I told him we couldn't talk until he figured this out. So I took a break from him and started doing my own thing. I even started talking to a new guy. He called me one day and asked me to come to his cousins house and chill with him. I agreed to go see him. When I got there, we talked about everything and agreed to move forward with one another. But I was l clear with him about taking everything one step at a time. I trusted him again. Afterwhile, everyone knew we were together again. His brothers loved me and his parents were aware that we were dating throughout the length of the relationship.

In the beginning, my mother was okay with everything. One day the pastor revealed a testimony about Amir and everything went left from there. I wasn't there to hear exactly what was said. Apparently, the pastor testified about Amir's near death experience. One day he collapsed and was later admitted to the

ICU. His family prayed for God to keep him alive. Prior to the collapse, he was living a street life; smoking, selling drugs, and living on the edge. By the time the information came to me, my mother was no longer okay with me dating him. She felt like he wasn't a good look for me. I didn't see his past as a reason to stop dating him. I defied her because I was an adult and I was going to date whomever I wanted to. So I did just that. I liked him and I didn't care what *anyone* had to say about it. My mother and I went back and forth about it a lot but I wasn't going to let her make this decision for me.

The first year of our relationship was cool. We hung out a lot. I wasn't much of a drinker before he and I met but after being around him, I did find myself drinking more than usual. Not only that, my drink of choice changed. Prior to him, I usually drank fruity drinks, nothing hard. After spending time with him, I started drinking *Tequila* and *Hennessey*. My mom noticed the change in me. She and I bumped heads about Amir often. I was sick of hearing it and I moved out as a result. I wasn't going to continue subjecting myself to the arguing especially when I knew I wasn't going to change my mind.

I know she didn't see what I saw in him. But when we began hanging out, I was able to see the *real* him. I wasn't judging him based on how he lived his life or based on the fact that he was the pastor's son. I liked his personality and the way he made me laugh. He showed me the kind of attention I wanted. He was honest (at least that's what I thought at the time). He loved me. I saw his potential. I knew he could be doing so much better than what he was doing at the time. He wasn't working a regular job. He was hustling drugs. One day, I told him that he needed to do better because I was working and in school.

Although I was working and in school, I managed to make sure I spent a considerable amount of time with him. I spent Thursday to Sunday with him and his family every week. When his parents traveled, they often asked him to check on their house and make sure he checked the mail. Little did they know, he delegated that task to me and I obliged. He'd give me the keys to their home and I did exactly what he asked. I found myself going the extra mile by picking up his nieces and nephews when their parents couldn't or when he was supposed to and refused since he was busy doing other things. I'd been knowing these people all my life, so I was happy to help. I didn't see anything wrong with what I was doing. I didn't think I was doing more than I should've been doing. When

I think about that, it reminds me of the saying, **"don't do wifely duties if you're not the wife."**

I moved in with a friend who was living around the corner from where Amir was periodically staying. Sometimes he'd stay with his cousins or at home with his parents. So he was here and there. But I was strictly at my friends house. Now that I was on my own, I needed to adjust to that new lifestyle. I applied for a personal loan so I could purchase a car. I was still in college, but I needed to get a job and I did. Looking back, I now know that I was making my life harder trying to be with this man.

The relationship continued going well. Then weird things started happening. His cousin's had their own house and we would kick it at their house often. One day while we were there, random women started showing up. I was playing it cool but in my mind I was thinking, *'who are these females?'* There was this particular girl who was extremely comfortable being in his face. She followed him from room to room. If I didn't know better, I'd think she was his girlfriend and not me. Truth is, I was never the kind of girl that was clingy with a man. But I'm *very* observant. I never said anything, I kept my cool.

One day I went to Target to apply for a job for him. (Yes, I said, "for him"). I took him back to take a test that was a part of the hiring process. He got an interview and was offered a job. Honestly, I thought I was doing my part. I was working mediocre jobs at the time. I couldn't afford to take care of him and me on my income. He needed to get a job. We only had one car so when I didn't have to work an early shift, I'd drop him off at work and vice versa.

One day I didn't have to work, but Amir said he did. So he drove himself to work and I stayed home to relax. It wasn't abnormal for Amir to have my car while I was working. From time to time, I'd notice certain things were missing from my car when he wasn't driving it. I used to have this gold nameplate necklace that I'd hang in my rearview mirror when I wasn't wearing it. Sometimes I'd get in the car and notice that the necklace was removed from the mirror and I'd always have to search the car for it. Another thing out of the ordinary was when I'd leave my purse in the backseat it was always missing. When I went to find it, it would be in the trunk. I honestly didn't think much of it at the time. At the time, I had a male best friend who was secretly in love with me (I found out much later). My best friend called me and told me he was outside my apartment and wanted to know if I was at home. I said I was and he asked me where my car was. I told him my boyfriend had the car because he had to work that day. He asked me to ride with him somewhere. I grabbed my keys and left with him. When I got in the car I asked him where we were going. He didn't answer me. He kept driving until we pulled up to my car that was sitting outside of someone's house. He parked alongside the car and asked me to climb over him and look in my car. When I looked in the window of my car, Amir was in it with another girl.

I LOST IT and immediately jumped out of the car to the passenger door where the girl was sitting. Unlucky for her, it wasn't locked so I opened the door and yanked the girl out by her hair. I kept hitting her in the face as she was screaming to the top of her lungs! I beat up the girl and popped him in the face, too. Amir pulled me off her and I finally came to myself and asked him why he was trying to save her. I told him he was disrespectful and they both could catch the bus. I got in my car and left! That was the first time I'd ever lost control of myself. It was like an out of body experience. I never knew I could get that upset. I was so hurt because I'd done so much to help him. Not that he needed me to because he had parents that had money but I'd spend money on clothes and shoes for him. He was my man and I wanted to do those things for him. I felt like if I'm looking good, you should be looking good too. If he needed money in his pocket, I made sure he had money in his pocket. I was doing my job as a good girlfriend, right? The least he could do was respect me and not entertain other females ESPECIALLY when he was supposed to be at work anyway…but I digress.

I was DONE with Amir! I was shaking as I was driving home. I called one of my girlfriends and told her what happened. She was so shocked I beat someone up. I wasn't the kind of person that believed in fighting to resolve *anything*. I never wanted to put my hands on anyone. I was a little upset with my best friend for bringing me to the scene instead of just telling me what he'd seen. That would've allowed me time to determine how I wanted to handle the situation. I felt like he put me in a bad position.

Once I got home, I was pacing the floor, shaking, and crying; *I was devastated.* I was so heartbroken that he'd cheated on me. I was going off cursing and crying in my house. I was rehearsing all of the things I'd done for him and the sacrifices

I'd made to be with him. That's when it dawned on me why my necklace and purse were never where I left them. He had the audacity to hide them so he could entertain other females! How did I let this happen? How could I let him make a fool of me like that? Even more disturbing, why did my "best friend" set me up? Amir didn't call for a couple of days, probably to keep calm because he was upset that I hit him. When he finally called, he apologized. I was in love with Amir so I forgave him. I gave him another chance. I wasn't thinking about how this situation was significantly similar to the situation that happened in the beginning of the relationship. I was young and I was thinking with my emotions, not logic.

The relationship continued and I was still doing a lot for him. He needed a phone so I took out an extra line on my cell phone plan so that he could have a phone. One night I was at my friend's house, we were getting ready to go out for the night. Before we left, I received a text message from some girl stating her name and letting me know that her and *my* boyfriend were back together. She continued to state that I wasn't anything to him, and I needed to back up. In fact, it was a group text to me and several other girls. What she didn't know was that message went to his sister, mother, and sister-in-law. The crazy part is, the message wasn't from the girl I found him in the car with, this was someone new. **This was just too much!**

I tried to brush the text message off and stay calm. I had been drinking so I just knew this wasn't what I thought this was. It *had* to be a joke. I gave the phone to my friend so she could read it for herself. She confirmed that the message was real so I called him immediately! The girl who sent the text message answered the phone yelling, cussing, calling me names, telling me not to call 'her man's phone.' I hung up on her, completely confused. Her man? Her man's phone? How so, when I'm paying the bill? I was starting to feel the same adrenaline rush and anger I felt during the car incident. I knew that night wasn't going to go well. My friend couldn't figure out why I was so calm; at least it looked that way on the outside. She told me, "If some chick answered my man's phone, I'd be in the car!" I needed to sort through my thoughts for a moment. After doing so, I called the phone back. She answered again with the same nonsense she did when I called the first time. I wasn't fond of her calling me out my name and she was beginning to piss me off. Out of nowhere, I started laughing which threw my friend off.

How dare Amir keep up this cheating charade after everything I'd done and was doing for him! I started crying in the midst of me laughing. I was angry as hell and I had a right to be. I stood up, grabbed my keys and told my friend that I knew where he was and that's where I was going. He was going to face me and so was she! Neither of them had a choice because before my friend could blink, I hit the door and was in my little black car. Before I turned the corner to the street where I knew he was, I turned my headlights off. I didn't want anyone to see me coming. I was positive he wasn't aware that the girl sent the messages or that she and I had encountered one another over the phone. So I was also sure that he didn't know I was coming to ruin everyone's night.

When I got there, I parked in front of the house next door to where he was and walked to the house he was in. The girl was standing outside in the driveway and I rushed her. She didn't even see it coming. I dragged that girl all over the driveway! I blacked out again. All I remember is one of his friends pulling me off her. Of course, she was talking crazy but she couldn't deny that she got whooped! I'm sure he heard the commotion because here he comes outside, yelling at me. I simply told him, "get out my face." I showed him the text messages as I was going off on him in front of everybody. I told him I couldn't do this anymore with him. I don't know if it was the liquor he was drinking but he was real cocky that night telling me that even if I left him, I'd come back. Since Amir was feeling himself that much, I snatched the phone that I was paying for and broke it in half. I told him that the service would be disconnected the next day.

We stood outside arguing and I threatened to hit him if he didn't get out of my face. I was serious about hitting him because I was just that angry. He wouldn't move so I started walking to my car and he followed me, antagonizing me. I wasn't scared to go to jail, I had bail money. He kept up the slick talking as I was getting in the car. Then he stood in front of the car and wouldn't allow me to leave. I told him to move and if he didn't I was going to hit him. He was insistent on standing there so I hit him with the car and he fell. I put the car in reverse and drove around him. He had a limp for a few days but he wasn't hurt too bad.

Even though I decided to go out with my friend, I still was upset, sad, and super emotional. My brain was all over the place. In the coming days the rage subsided and the hurt set in. I cried a lot. I couldn't believe he was cheating yet again and allowed someone to disrespect me. Why did he think it was okay to treat me this way when I've sacrificed so much to be with him? I chose him over my mother and now I was suffering the consequence. This is exactly what she was trying to save me from and I couldn't see it at the time she was saying it but as the cheating continued, I thought a lot about how she tried to warn me. I knew I had to break up with him indefinitely. I'd lost myself in him. It shouldn't have gone that far. I was beginning to see how my relationship with him was changing me. I became more violent. I drank more. I was angrier. I'd always been a sweet, caring person and the change in me was overshadowing that. I forgot my worth. I lost my self-esteem. My mother and grandfather always taught me that I should be loved unconditionally and I lost sight of that behind this man.

I didn't talk to Amir for two days. He was calling but I wasn't answering. At the time, I had the willpower to stay away from him. I started seeing other people in an attempt to move on from him. Then I started feeling sick. My breast began hurting and I was vomiting, so I went to *Planned Parenthood* and completed a pregnancy test. It came back negative. After that, I attended a funeral and saw my cousin there who took one good look at me and said, "you're pregnant." I said, "no I'm not." I couldn't be. It had been months since my ex and I were intimate. So I went back to Planned Parenthood a week later and took another pregnancy test. This time the test came back positive. I was shocked. How could I take two pregnancy tests within two weeks and the results be opposite? The clinician informed me that the first test could've come back negative for a number of reasons; the time of day, hormones, etc.

It was 2008 and Amir and I had been broken up for several months. But with the news of the pregnancy, I had no choice but to call him. When I called, I told him we needed to talk because I was pregnant. He told me he was going to call me back and hung up the phone. I didn't hear from him. That in itself was yet another wake up call. I had hoped that even though we were no longer together, he and I would work things out for the sake of our child. But his reaction killed my hope. I had to go to my mother and tell her that I was pregnant. When I revealed the news to her, she was so hurt. She didn't speak to me for two months. She felt like it was a poor lapse in judgement. At the time, my cousin and I decided it was best if I came to live with him and his girlfriend so I could be in a more stable environment. I started a new position at a daycare. My aunts came to town and had a conversation with my mother. After convincing her that it was best if we dealt with this as a family, they asked me to come home and I did.

I was one of the few of my family members that went to college and had life goals. I didn't just have goals, I was actually achieving them. So when I found out I was pregnant, I felt a deep sense of disappointment in myself. *How was I going to finish school?* I felt like I was doomed to the same life everyone else in my family had. I wanted *more* and I wasn't sure how I would get it being a single mother. I was feeling embarrassed and it felt like I had to tell everyone in my life one by one that I was pregnant. Everyone had an opinion or tried to give me advice about what my next move should be. I didn't want to be a single mother. I wanted to break the generational curse in my family.

It was odd coming back home as a pregnant woman. I didn't have a bed at my mother's house. I was sleeping on the couch. Being back home, I was even more embarrassed. My younger brother was in high school at the time and he was supportive of me but I could feel the difference in the way he saw me. I was no longer the example that I should've been.

I had a miserable pregnancy. I was very sad during that time. Amir eventually came around trying to be reassuring but also telling his parents that my child wasn't his. His parents were also claiming they didn't even know their son and I were dating. Which was a total lie. *They knew everything.* I was definitely no stranger to them. This information came to me by way of the first lady of the church. The first lady told me I was ruining my life and wanted me to apologize to the church for being pregnant. I was considered a church public figure. I was involved in a lot of activities in the church and mostly everyone knew who I was. They felt like I owed the congregation an apology. Yet, there were other women who were just as involved in the church as I was, if not, more and they weren't asked to do the same thing. I wasn't going to explain, apologize, or profess my sins to anyone. I didn't care what she said. Some may call it disrespect, I call it self-respect.

I was hurt and appalled at the audacity of her acting as if I created this baby by myself. When I walked out of her office, my view of her changed drastically.

I never looked at her the same. I used to hold her in high regard. Now, she's just another person to me. Throughout the pregnancy, I felt alone. My first ultrasound was coming up and my ex said he'd attend the appointment with me. I went to pick him up and he never came outside. He left me sitting outside for an hour! During my first doctor's appointment, I was tested for all STDs, including HIV. My test for STDs came back positive for Chlamydia which is contracted from men. I wasn't having sex with *anyone*. In fact, he was the last person I'd been with. I called him immediately and went off! That was the last conversation I had with him throughout the rest of my pregnancy.

While I was pregnant, my grandparents were having health challenges. I struggled with that on top of being pregnant. No matter how hard I tried to be happy, I was miserable. Sometimes my mother would pray over my stomach for my baby's health and happiness. My family decided to have a baby shower and my cousin was going to be the organizer. I invited everyone to the baby shower, even Amir's parents. I wasn't being petty. I truly wanted them to be there. Inviting his parents ruined what little peace I had left.

When they received the invite, it wasn't the parents that contacted me. It was one of the other family members and she tried to be nice about it. But I knew that under all that sweet talk, his parents were truly seething about my pregnancy. His parents wanted to hide the pregnancy as much as possible, hence the reason they denied knowing anything about me and Amir.

I'd gotten sick towards the end of my pregnancy. I was losing color in my face, my feet were so swollen that I couldn't wear shoes. My mother knew something was wrong and took me to the ER. When I got there I had to be induced. I was in labor for 4 days, from Feb. 26 to March 1, 2009 via c-section. Amir didn't come to the hospital while I was in labor. My mom received a call from my aunt who delivered some hurtful news. Apparently, Amir was at the hospital with another woman while she was also giving birth to his child. I had no room to be in my feelings. I had to focus on having a healthy baby. I wish my mother would've waited to give me the news. I didn't need to hear that at that time. There would've been no perfect time to deliver news like that but there was a better time to do it.

While I was in labor, one of Amir's cousins came and sat with me until I had the baby. I was very grateful for her presence. My mother, brother, and cousin were also there with me. Thank God my daughter arrived safely. She was a preemie, 5lbs, 6oz. And had jaundice. Her body temperature kept dropping and she accidentally swallowed some of her own feces. Her stomach had to be pumped to remove the feces and the doctors also checked for any infection. There was so much going on but having my daughter was the best experience of my life. I did text Amir to let him know that she was born. Although I was hurt, I did put his parents on the list for visitation just in case they had a change of heart. But no one came. They were still denying my daughter. Amir finally showed up, high as ever. The first thing that came out of his mouth when he arrived was, "when are we getting a DNA test?" He hadn't even looked at her or picked her up. I told him to get out of my room.

I was finally released to go home two days after giving birth and my mother was being a true new grandmother. She sent a picture of my daughter to **everyone.** The doctor had some concerns about the baby. Apparently she was showing signs of spina bifida and we had to take her to a specialist. So I wasn't able to go home and heal from the c-section. I was completely overwhelmed and worried about her. My mother talked to the bishop of the church who asked that we bring the baby to church next Sunday so he could pray over her. After prayer, I left immediately.

Amir and I had a pregnancy scare before the pregnancy and birth of my daughter. At that time I told him that I'd never put him on child support as long as he was supportive during my pregnancy and a consistent father after the baby was born. With this pregnancy he showed me exactly the type of man he was going to be. So when I filed for child support, I also petitioned the court for a DNA test. He was late for that appointment and the officials were ready to issue a bench warrant for his arrest. I called him several times and when he finally answered, he wanted me to give them an excuse for his tardiness. Even though he was en route, I covered him, but I was irritated that once again, I had to save him.

I found out that Amir moved out of town to Stevens Point, WI with his cousin. At the time I was keeping him informed about our daughter via text messages. I wanted to make sure I was making the effort for her sake. So I drove to Stevens Point so he could see his daughter. She was about 6 months old. When I went to visit him, I still had feelings of wanting a family. I was still determined to break the generational curse in my family. Amir and I mutually agreed to give our relationship another try. I didn't want my daughter to grow up in a broken home.

For the first 6 months of my daughter's life, I stayed home so she and I could bond. No work, no school. When the 6 months ended, I went back to school and got a job working for the *Boys and Girls Club*. Amir came back to Milwaukee to live with his parents and also got a job working for the Club. Afterwhile, I was able to get a one bedroom apartment for my daughter and myself. Amir also moved out of his parents house and got an apartment with one of his cousins. Things were going well. If he needed help with his half of the rent, I was there to help him. Amir stayed at my place with the baby and I every other day.

When my daughter was 8 months old, Amir's mother saw me at a church meeting and asked to see the baby. At that moment, the baby was with my mother in a private room in the church. It felt odd because I hadn't kept up with his family in over a year. I went to the room and told my mom that his mother wanted to see the baby. She frowned, so I knew she was against it. When his mother came in she cooed over my daughter and told me how beautiful she was. After meeting my daughter for the first time, his mother told me she wanted to spend more time with the baby. My mother felt like the change of heart was only coming from the paternity test results they'd received in the mail but she told me to do what I felt was right on my heart. I have to say, his parents stepped up and since then, have been a big help; more of a help than her own father has.

During the course of us trying to maintain our family, there were no signs of cheating and everything seemed to be going well. Then I started having consistent, vivid dreams about him cheating with a particular woman. I remembered exactly what the woman looked liked and the kind of conversation she and I were having in the dream. I even knew her name. I know it sounds crazy, but it's true. It just so happens that the woman I was dreaming about was the same woman who was following him around at his cousin's house several years back. So I asked him if he was talking to a girl named Tanae. His mouth dropped and I *knew* he was about to lie….and he did. He said they were "just friends". I already knew from experience that the truth would prevail. I just needed to keep myself calm until it did.

One day my brother fell ill with meningitis and I was scared for his life. My mother, my daughter and I were at the hospital waiting for an update from the doctors. While waiting, my mother told me to go home and she'd stay at the hospital. A friend of mine came to pick me up and I asked her to take me back to Amir's house. When I arrived, I noticed his bedroom was a mess. He'd just bought a new bed frame and stuff was everywhere. I didn't want my daughter to hurt herself so I began picking things up and putting them in his closet while he was in the living room with the baby. As I was doing so, I saw a sweater in his closet with a name on it, *Becky from the Block*. He'd thrown her clothes in the closet thinking I wouldn't find them. I'd noticed some female belongings at his apartment before and it was enough to make me pause, but I thought they belonged to his cousin's girlfriend. I didn't say anything. I was calm, but I knew I had to get out of there before I had another black out moment. I refused to act a fool in front of my daughter. I played it cool until he left to grab pizza for dinner. The moment he closed the door, I immediately called my cousin to pick me up. I was still calm, but I was also **done**. When I got home, I texted Amir and told him that I'd found Tanae's clothes in his closet and that I already knew something was going on because I'd been dreaming about him cheating with her for several weeks. I told him that I wanted my family but I was no longer going to allow him to hurt me. I also told him that when he wanted to see our daughter, he was welcome to call and I'd drop her off and pick her up. I never allowed myself to be with him again.

It hurt me so bad that he was choosing to continue being sneaky. I know we weren't married but he made a commitment to me and our daughter to do right by us. It hurt my soul to find out that he was still up to no good. I was so in love with Amir. But I had to take some ownership. I saw the signs and I kept trying to be with him. Of course, he made it seem like I was crazy. He tried to flip everything on me. But I bypassed that drama. **I was done**. A few days later, Amir contacted me saying he wanted to see our daughter. The day he wanted to see her, I had a whole day planned with her and my family. But I wanted to be fair so I took her to see him for a few hours. Just when I thought things couldn't get worse, they did.

When I arrived at his apartment, I put the baby and her bag on the bed and said I was leaving. I told Amir I'd be back in an hour to pick her up. He asked me to stay so we could talk. But I wasn't having it and I made myself clear that we were done. **No more talking.** I told him that if it wasn't about our daughter, there wasn't anything for us to discuss. He was still persistent about wanting to talk. He said I was always disrespecting him when he wanted to talk. As I was walking out the door he grabbed my arm and everything went left from there. He beat me up right in front of our daughter.

His roommates were there and didn't stop him. When I was able to grab my daughter and head towards the door, he kicked me in my back. I called my friend who lived across the street. She rushed over to his house. She walked with me to a nearby fire department, who took pictures of my wounds, read the text messages he was sending me and called the police department. I went to the hospital that night. My hip was knocked out of place and I had a back and pelvic injury. I had to complete two minor surgeries and attend therapy for months. Due to the domestic violence I experienced that day, I now have arthritis in my spine to this day.

The District Attorney pressed charges against Amir. When I went to court, the judge wanted to place a 10 year restraining order on him but I wouldn't allow that for the sake of my daughter. No matter what happened between him and I, I didn't want her to grow up without her father. She deserved better than that.

Since then I've forgiven Amir. I still have flashbacks of the incident, especially when the pain resurfaces. I had to do a lot of soul-searching after the beating. It was a very chaotic year. I remember my sister asking me 4 life-changing questions prior to the incident about Amir and I want you to ask yourself the same questions when you are assessing whether or not you should waste your time being with a guy:

1. **Why are you attracted to him?**
2. **If you love him, why do you love him?**
3. **Does he treat you the way you need and should be treated?**
4. **If you were in trouble or stranded and needed him would he be there?**

I knew I loved Amir but he had never treated me well. He told me he loved me, but I don't really think he knew what love was. He had never been there for me even though I literally gave my life to him. I realized I was attracted to being a part of his family and us building a family together. I knew I had to let Amir go once and for all. So I did.. Later on, he sent me an email apologizing for everything he'd ever done to me. I was shocked and relieved. I cried because I'd been waiting for an apology for so long. I didn't think it was ever going to come and I'd accepted that.

After some much needed healing and time spent alone, I met Matt. He and I began dating and we got pregnant but unfortunately miscarried. He wasn't too happy about me being pregnant anyway. As the relationship continued, I found out that he was seeing other people and I was hurt by that. Matt and I cared for each other deeply, but our core values about life were completely different. He had no interest in healing his inner wounds. I'm about healing the brokenness. As I was dating Matt, I felt like I was toxic to him. I still had a lot of healing to do. We broke up and I used that time as an opportunity to heal further. He stayed in my life and ended up helping me heal through a particular stage in my life. Matt has also become a lifetime friend that I'm grateful for.

While dating Amir, I suffered so much pain because I didn't listen to wisdom. I overlooked a lot and I didn't make decisions that served my best interest. <u>As a single mother who is dating or you desire to date, please be cautious and pay attention to the following:</u>

1. **Listen to the wise people in your life**. Had I listened to my mother, I would've made better decisions and left him sooner.
2. **When a person shows you who they are, believe them**. Don't keep repainting the red flag green, thinking the result will be different. A person doesn't change unless *they* want to.
3. **Know your worth**. Walk away from the men who don't deserve your attention so that you're not exhausted when the right one comes along
4. **When you're dating, give your children room to be themselves.** The last thing you want is for them to end up being rebellious because you're being entirely too strict due to your own past trauma or insecurities.

Due to my horrific experience with Amir, I am now able to see the red flags I ignored. I can also admit when I'm wrong. I never should have ignored the girl following him around the house. I never should have left the safety of my mother's house. I grew up very sheltered so I wanted to do what I wanted to do. While my daughter is not a mistake, I had the opportunity to make better choices, but I chose Amir instead. While my intentions were good, the relationship was bad for me. I didn't know my worth at the time, but now I do and I know who I am. I have enough strength to walk away from the things and people that don't serve me. I am determined to teach my daughter to do the same.

If you're not receiving the treatment you deserve, you have a duty to yourself to walk away. It makes no sense to sit in any relationship and allow someone to mistreat you. There is no settling for less! I had to re-evaluate myself. I realized I was looking for a daddy in a man and I had to come to the realization that no man that I'm involved with romantically can fill the void of my absent father. I was suffering from a broken heart and didn't even know it. I needed to detach myself from all levels of drama so I could heal from my pain. I'm still uncovering a lot of my daddy issues, so right now I'm all about me. I know that I'm not good for *any* man at this time. When I do decide to start dating again, I'm going to be ready. I want to be able to present the best version of myself. I'm not in a rush to be in love. I'm in a rush to love myself. It takes time to break down old trauma. Give yourself that time to acknowledge, address, and heal from those old wounds. I'm not perfect. I'm still learning. I'm still growing. I'm still forgiving myself and others. Understand that forgiveness is not for the other person, it's for you and your growth. You'll be that much better of a partner, communicator, mate, and wife when you take the time to heal first.

"Being a single mother doesn't mean you're handicapped. But it does mean you have to do more work. Don't use your children as an excuse but as a reason to do better."

~ AJEYA HONGO

A Reason to Win

By: Ajeya Hongo

I know all too well how difficult single mom life can be. We're always concerned and consumed with one thing or another. I know that one of the biggest stress factors of being a single parent is income. Oftentimes, single mothers are left to carry the financial load of taking care of themselves and their children. While I was building my network marketing career, I was a single mother. I experienced the trials and tribulations of dating and looking for a partner. Since building my career I've come in contact with single mothers that have questions and need coaching. I've been able to assist single mothers by teaching them how to stop relying on child support by encouraging them to provide better lives for their children.

I have an amazing 5-year-old daughter from a previous relationship. Even though I am currently in a relationship, I had certain standards in place when I was dating. I was strict about who met my daughter. I never saw my mom with random men so I conducted myself in the same way. Ladies, when you're out here dating, don't assume every man you meet is fit to step in and play daddy to your children. Be choosy with who has the right to meet your children.

While my current relationship is wonderful, I had some issues I needed to work on. I have a dominant personality, which has caused problems for me in my past relationships. I'm used to doing things on my own and being in control. My mother was independent; she was the one who taught me how to hustle to take care of myself. Since I've been in this relationship, I've had to learn how to be more submissive and let go of the reigns. I had to let him be a man. It took time, but I learned how to lean back and allow him to handle masculine tasks such as taking out the trash and carrying the groceries inside. Ladies, I know we can do those things, but it's okay let him do it.

In retrospect, I wish I'd known then what I know now. I went through hell before I became aware of my true purpose in life. On Valentine's Day 2014, I met up with some friends for dinner and met my daughter's father, Nick, through our mutual friends. After dinner, we went back to my friend's place to hang out. He and I were enjoying each other's company and getting to know each other. I thought he was cute, smart, and I liked that he was tall. At the time, I thought he was a hustler. I liked that about him as well because I've always been about having my own. When I saw that he matched me in that area, I was much more interested in him. We moved quickly from that night forward. Three months later we were in a committed relationship and I'd gotten pregnant. I was afraid to tell my parents because I was only 20-years-old and knew they'd be disappointed. When I told Nick, he was calm about it. He didn't mind that I was pregnant. He didn't give me any problems, so I thought we would make great parents. Little did I know, he was about to show his true colors.

My pregnancy changed my life. I began to develop a different perspective about life and what responsibility truly meant. He and I moved into his mother's house because of the pregnancy and stayed there until shortly after my daughter was born. When I brought up the suggestion of us looking for a place for when the baby was born, he always had an excuse. We were only in year one, and I already knew our relationship was over; however, I stayed for another 3 years. Over the course of the relationship, I slowly began finding myself.

About eight months into my pregnancy, the truth began to reveal itself. I found out that he was entertaining other women. One night while he was rubbing my stomach, a text message came through on his phone. I looked at the phone and saw the hearts that someone sent him. I asked him who it was. He refused to answer me. He didn't want to make a scene in his mom's home so we went into another room. I asked him to give me his phone, and he refused. He eventually opened the phone and showed me all the text messages from other women. All I could do was laugh. I was past the crying phase. Oftentimes we become afraid to start over. We look at the time we've invested in a person and assume that's a good enough reason to stay. Even though we're sacrificing our true desires, boundaries, and happiness, we settle because we don't want to be alone.

Nick was a big-time social media user. So I thought it was strange that he never mentioned me or the pregnancy on social media. **Red Flag!** When I asked him why he never posted a picture of me, his response was, "I have posted you."When he showed me the picture he posted, it was a picture from two years prior. There was always an excuse and we always argued about social media. I felt like he was using social media to fool around. Being in a relationship and expecting your first child are monumental phases of life. The only reason he wouldn't mention those things is because he was hiding me from other women.

Before I got into network marketing, I was in the credit restoration business. Nick and I decided to move to Las Vegas and were able to secure our own apartment. This was my first apartment and I wanted to make sure we were able to keep up and not lose our new place. Although my credit restoration business was making money, I still went out and found a job. Living with him was no cakewalk. He wasn't contributing to our financial responsibilities and he always left me to figure things out on my own. He saw me running my business and working a job, and he just watched. He refused to do anything to lighten the load for me. I began to wonder, *what are you here for?* He was of no use to me. I was taking care of myself, my daughter, *and* a grown man. Realizing this was a pivotal moment. This is when I knew I was done.

While I was with Nick, it was as if I was a single parent. He didn't help in the way I needed him to. I had to be the man and the woman in the relationship and over time, that became exhausting. I couldn't keep it up any longer. I believe a man is supposed to prioritize his family. As my relationship continued, the fighting became more frequent. Every time I tried to hold him accountable, he'd start an argument. It was getting to the point where I couldn't stand the sight of him. One of our fights was so bad that someone called the police. I knew then that I was no longer in a position to be selfish. I couldn't stay in this relationship like this. I had to think about my daughter's safety. He didn't want to leave so he decided to stay in the apartment. I decided to take my daughter and go. We stayed with a friend of mine before heading back to my mom's in California. We didn't stay there long. I was just waiting for my application for another apartment complex in Las Vegas to be approved. Once I got the call that my application was approved, my daughter and I went back to Las Vegas and moved into our own apartment. That was the end of my relationship with Nick. I can't be sure that I was ever really in love with him. Sometimes we think it's love that we feel when it's actually infatuation, attachment, or sheer lust.

From the moment that I left, he hasn't been an active parent in our daughter's life. One Christmas, I went back home to California to be with my family. I agreed to meet up with his mother so she could see my daughter. He popped up, arms full of gifts, and he hadn't seen our daughter in 2 years. **I was furious.** After that, I got a message from Nick asking me to go to dinner. I shut that down quickly. I told him that all we needed to focus on was co-parenting. I also explained to him that he couldn't just pop up when he wanted to. He needed to be consistently present or consistently absent. But riding the fence wasn't an option. He promised us he'd be more present. There was a moment when they'd talk often, then he disappeared. Even his mother was frustrated with his actions. When she tried to speak to him about it, he disrespectfully told her that he'd call my daughter when he felt like it. I knew it was time to cut off all communication. I had to protect her in any way I possibly could and his disrespect was not welcomed. I wasn't afraid to be alone or start over. That's a part of the journey of life. Anyone that has a difficult time respecting their parents, is going to also have a difficult time respecting you.

There was a time in my life where I was close-minded to different things. Since the split with Nick, I've learned that women have to be open-minded to new opportunities. I also learned that I had to be connected to a circle of people who lived the kind of life I wanted. It's okay to explore your desires and reinvent yourself. That's what growth is. I never placed Nick on child support. I don't believe in that. Many single moms are programmed to think that we need two incomes in one household to be financially secure. That's not true. We're programmed to believe we have to put our children's fathers on child support. Also, not true. I don't think single moms realize it, but putting a man on child support adds to the pain you're already carrying. Sometimes it's better to break the bond completely, suck it up, and do what you have to do for the betterment of you and your children.

No one wants to go through heartbreak and loss. No one would take that route if there were another option. But usually, that's the only way you're able to step into your purpose. Your life's work is usually attached to the things you've struggled with. I lost so much while I was with my daughter's father. My car got repossessed and I'd gotten evicted back-to-back. It was a lesson learned, but if I didn't go through all the turmoil of my previous relationship, it would be impossible for me to help other single mothers. I'm grateful for the growth it pushed me to. I know what I deserve. Now, I am in a relationship with someone worth holding on to, and we've been together for three years.

While you're healing, learning, and coming into the new you, make sure you have your fundamental needs in check. Get your credit and finances together! It doesn't matter if you have a college degree; if your credit is not together, you're limiting yourself. As I began working on my credit, new opportunities became available to me. Finances and credit go hand-in-hand. If you're focused on getting your credit intact, you should also be looking for ways to increase your income. There are plenty of avenues of income besides relying on child support. Do your research and see what additional streams of income will be a good fit for you. If you have a passion that can turn into another stream of income, explore that. Don't be selfish. If you're not going to explore other avenues of income for yourself, then do it for your children. Being a single mother doesn't mean you're handicapped. It simply means you have to do more work. Don't use your children as an excuse to fail, but as a reason to win.

"Stop looking for a man. What's supposed to happen will happen. You don't have to be on the hunt for anything!"

~ Dr. Earleen Parson-Ross

Cut To The Chase!

By: Dr. Earleen Parson-Ross

*M*any times people think there's one road to success, one road to healing, and one way to reach a goal. But I believe that our journeys are tailor-made to fit each of us individually. There's no mold to fit. We're all going to make mistakes. It's inevitable. But the best part of the mistake is how you learn and grow from it. Introspection has always been my personal goal. It's what makes us better people for ourselves, those around us, and those that will enter our lives at a later date. I know that as a single mother, you can get wrapped up in the needs of your children and forget your own, but you have to take care of yourself. One of the biggest cautions for a single mother is her dating life. Those of us that have been there or are currently living that life, we know how difficult and strenuous that can be. It's a thoughtful balancing act, and it is imperative that single mothers use wisdom when dating.

I was married to my husband for 16 years before we separated. It was quite a journey. I was a single mother when we met. My daughter was 7 years old and he had a daughter who was 3. He was very intelligent and intriguing. I need intellectual stimulation, so the friendship was satisfying and natural. We'd talk about anything from politics to mind and body congruence. He and I were both spiritual teachers so we had a lot of spiritual conversations as well. It was important to me not to forfeit my need for spiritual compatibility. It was also important that the man that I would be with would possess the qualities necessary to father my young daughter.

Prior to giving birth to my daughter, I would not date a man who had children. After having my daughter, I would not date a man that did not have a child. Just like that – becoming a mother drastically changed my dating criteria. There's a difference between being a single person and a single parent. As important as dating may be, the needs and safety of a single mother's minor children are not only essential, but also top priority. I dated several men while my daughter was young, but she only remembers two "legitimate boyfriends". Although I was not without error, I was careful not to bring men into my daughter's space and life until I felt that it was safe, and until I was confident that the relationship had a propitious future. I don't take full credit for that virtue – I learned it from my mother. My mother became a widow with eight children when I was just 18 months. Throughout my childhood I only recall my mother having one "boyfriend". When I grew older she explained that she was very particular about "having men around her children". This may seem extreme to some, but this was not uncommon practice way back then in the 60's. So even in the 90's, that protective, provisional instinct kicked in, and I followed suit.

Before moving forward with words of wisdom and recommendations for dating as a single mom, I would like to share some of the errors and poor choices I made, and yellow flags that I ignored. My intention is to not only "help" you, but also to convey my humanness, as not to portray a super-saint who has all of the answers. The personal examples that I divulge are for the purpose of practical illustration and to substantiate the recommendations. I don't believe that there's a woman on earth who hasn't had relationship-bloopers, and embarrassing outbursts and behaviors that they regret. Even with good up-bringing and wholesome people in your life, single mothers can and do make unwise decisions concerning dating. Why? There's no single reason, but amongst them are desperation, curiosity, peer-pressure, lack of self-awareness, greed, rebellion, lack of self-esteem, impatience, and naivety.

Yellow Flag #1: ignoring the caliber of woman his ex wives/girlfriends were
Yellow Flag # 2: while he was still married, he came on to me
Yellow Flag # 3: negative talk about his current or past significant other
Yellow Flag # 4: ignoring cycles and patterns of erratic behavior
Yellow Flag # 5: substitution of apologies and discussions with expensive gifts

There are essential considerations to which single mothers should adhere when deciding to date. First of all, honesty is key. We must truthfully decide whether or not we are "ready" to date. **Readiness** is substantially determined by how your last relationship ended, when it ended, and how it left you feeling about both yourself, and relationships in general. When we end one relationship and enter into another too quickly, we often contaminate the new relationship with residue of previous one. This is not uncommon for people to do, as they often attempt to skip the grief process of the last relationship and numb themselves with new affection. These relationships rarely ever last. I recommend doing the work necessary to prepare yourself for a fruitful and lasting relationship. What work? I'm glad you asked. After readiness comes the question of **lessons learned**. I believe that with every adventure in life, there's a lesson to be learned. When relationships end, we are often so preoccupied with blame, revenge and sorrow, that we seldom take time to find out what we can do differently next time. We must also ask ourselves *why* **we desire to date**. (True story: one of my coworkers once said, "I need a man... I need a second income.") We must be honest enough to determine whether our desire is merely sex, adult attention, financial assistance, company and companionship, a father-figure for our children, or something else. There's nothing wrong with wanting any or all of those things, but what's consequential is the manner in which we obtain them. To attempt to fulfill a hidden agenda under the guise of a relationship is just flat out wrong (whether men do it, or whether women do it). In this day and age, there are plenty of consensual "transactional relationships", so there's really no need for deception and manipulation. At the risk of making dating sound academic, I also believe that there should be **relationship goals**. You should know your goals. Your significant other should know your goals. You should know your significant other's goals, and your significant other should know his own goals. At this juncture of your life (a grown woman with at least one child), time is too precious to gamble with assumptions. It's acceptable to have different personal goals, but your relationship goals should be congruent. Another major consideration is the **impact the relationship will have on your child(ren)**. The child's age is a key factor of this consideration, and will give cause to their reaction. Also, if you decide to bring a male friend into your children's space and they don't like him... put your defenses away and find out why! The opinions of adult children about your dating prospects can be a two-edged sword.

I had a full life before I got married, and after marrying I had another child, so my life changed very quickly. I thought that I had a good understanding of healthy compromise, however somewhere along the way, I put my goals on hold and lost myself. Of course I did not realize that I'd lost myself in the many additional roles that I'd taken on after marriage, until I was submerged in the frustration that accompanied it. One Sunday in the days leading up to the separation, my daughter came over. She looked at her deteriorating mother and said, "You're better than this. Don't forget who you are." (My daughter loved her stepdad, but she and I had ten years together before I married. She experienced a strong, independent woman prior to his arrival.) When she left the house, I wept. I had to find myself again. She told me not to forget who I was, but it was too late. I had already long forgotten who I used to be, and I didn't know when it happened.

With this disclosure, my recommendation is to always **keep your finger on the pulse of your sense of self and personal goals** – regardless of your desired level of dating and commitment. Goals, desires, needs, and priorities change as life progresses, and you reserve the right to change your mind. Thus, we must purposefully and periodically evaluate ours without fear, hesitation or regret.

At some point in life, most of us have stated something that we would never do or would never "put up with" in a relationship; and most of us have done and/or "put up with" those exact things. It is especially easy to make such declarations when talking about someone else's relationship. The first purpose of this statement is to emphasize that we should never say what we would never do. Most people have (or should have) relationship deal-breakers. Regardless of whether or not we actually live by them, **we should have principles and standards by which we live**. Experiences and time passed teach us many lessons about ourselves and about life itself. Our responsibility is to be alert and heed the lessons. This prevents us from getting stuck on the treadmill of resembling, failed relationships.

The other purpose of that statement is to confess one of my own humbling examples of it. Sometimes we don't know ourselves as well as we think we do. When my (then) husband came to me and said he didn't want to make it work anymore, his words echoed in the air and shook me to my core! They literally snatched the wind out of me. My pride wouldn't permit me to beg him to stay because I was too "strong a woman" for that. A few weeks later, I dismissed my pride, and yielded to what was the most humiliating act that I can ever remember executing… I begged him to stay. It took me about two weeks to convince myself that it was okay to do that; afterall, he used to tell me that I did not "honor" him enough. Well, I couldn't think of a more abased endeavor. Here was my colossal attempt to prove to him that I *did* honor him. When my act of humility proved to be futile, the strong woman within mocked me for making a fool of myself. Contrary to the strong woman's perspective, the virtuous woman within applauded me, and assured me that I'd done all that I could to fight for my marriage. She assured me that in days and weeks to come, and through the tears, hurt and pain, I would have peace, not ever having to wonder if there was anything else that I could have done to make it work. I had to emotionally withdraw from my ex as best as I could. It was a complex process but I steadily began detaching myself. Despite the marital problems, I didn't want to divorce. There was something inimical about hearing the love of my life tell me that he didn't want to be with me anymore, that awakened a surge of self-worth, purpose and determination within me. It hit differently when I heard him say those words. He and I were a dynamic couple, but I'd done all I could do to salvage the marriage.

We were public figures in our own right, and thus had a public marriage. Naturally, people feel entitled to know the truth and details when or if things go wrong. While I believe that some type of statement is in order, I also believe that no one outside the marriage is **entitled** to know anything. With this I segway to the recommendation that **we must allow ourselves as much time as it takes to Heal!** Don't try to heal too quickly, date too quickly, or explain too quickly. We can never completely mitigate gossip, judgment, speculation, lies or rumors, but we often (knowingly and unknowingly) contribute to the nonsense when we speak while in our pain. No one wants their transgressions to be exposed, and oftentimes in our vulnerability, we divulge particulars that should be protected. I decided to remove myself from social media altogether. I did that so that I would not be provoked to respond to any of the foolery that crept up on my timeline, and subsequently "give a dog a bone". We've all seen people attempt to hash out their differences (especially break-ups) in the court of social media. I was determined not to indulge. So if I didn't see the nonsense, I couldn't be lured into the ring of foolishness. I was already broken and depressed; I wouldn't use my energy to fight people that didn't even matter. And while I'm being completely transparent, I was feeling some kind of way toward God. Yes, I said it! I prayed, fasted and begged God to restore my marriage. "How dare He allow my marriage to fall apart?! He had the power to fix it!" Well, the details of that chapter are far too much to indulge in this writing, but God obviously got me straight. I apologized, and He didn't hold my idiocy against me. I had to remind myself that worse things have happened to better people. In the beginning of the separation, I was all about isolation; I just didn't want to be bothered. As I began healing, the isolation became solitude. I was deliberately seeking the presence of God alone. I heard from Him in such a way that I never would have heard otherwise. When I was healed enough, I reclaimed my life, and even got back on social media. It took time and discipline, but after 16 years of marriage, I had to recalibrate my life. It took additional time to fight the feelings of bitterness and anger towards my ex.

One day, I hung up the phone after speaking with my ex and noticed that my bitterness was gone. It felt odd that I wasn't angry, especially because I had a valid reason to be upset with him. Then it hit me. I remembered praying to God for help with forgiving anyone that had ever offended or harmed me. The light came on and I realized that this was an answered prayer. I was grateful that I wasn't carrying the weight of unforgiveness anymore. I felt so much lighter. A burden had been lifted and a sense of freedom replaced it. So many of us are addicted to our pain. Even when God heals us from the wounds, we tend to revert back to the negativity because we're accustomed to it. When we choose not to forgive, we are asserting covert control over others. We seem to feel more powerful when we're holding someone by the neck about what they've done to us. I had to surrender my right to be angry in order to embrace the liberty of forgiveness. I have taken the time to reflect on my role in the dissipation of my marriage. Far too often, we point the finger at the other person. We want to say that we were blameless and our ex was the destructive party. But a mature person knows that "it takes two", and each must be responsible enough to acknowledge his or her part. I am identifying where I've grown, and how both the marriage and the divorce have helped to shape me. I believe that men need to feel needed, and in retrospect, I could have done more to make my husband feel needed. I also vow not to punish the next man for my ex-husband's shortcomings. I have to be healed enough to give the next man a clean slate.

Dating as a single mom this time (more than 20 years later) is done with a different approach. I know who I am, I have greater insight, different needs and desires, my children are grown, and I have different goals. Needless to say that the dating scene has drastically changed since my last indulgence. Ironically, I occasionally encounter men who still use the same trendy pick-up lines that I remember hearing when I was single 20 and 30 years ago. My 21st Century dating escapades have shorter lifespans than the ones from days of old. There's a good reason for that… I am more attentive, and I no longer disregard the yellow flags. Also, my confidence to address contradictory and/or questionable behavior is intact. For example, I recently ended a relationship. This gentleman and I consciously decided to get to know one another. I was both pleased and impressed with the relationship's pace and quality. Weighty, differing political views were at the center of the wedge that pushed us apart. That may sound insequential, but believe me when I say that it was quite significant. This is especially true in this current economic and political climate that has hijacked practically every headline, breaking story, social media post, phone conversation, billboard, and pulpit commentary. There were many things that we liked about one another, but the deal breaker was the character/personality that his political allegiance created. It was something that I absolutely could not tolerate, as it began to bleed into every aspect of the relationship. I don't argue religion or politics, and it seemed as if his entire mission was to disprove any and every opposing view. The daily conversations completely exhausted me. Whew!

Another experience that I'd like to share is about a young man that I referred to as "Drug". I've chosen to share this encounter for two reasons: 1. The impact of the relationship was incredibly regenerating, and it caught me unaware. 2. It demonstrates implementation of the recommendations that I've mentioned. The condensed version is that within a short period of time, this man and I developed a very strong mutual affection. He was super intelligent, witty, mature, spiritually sound, attractive, and attentive. I honestly don't have words to express our connection; it was like finding a missing puzzle piece. I was very happy. I nicknamed him Drug because the influence he had on me was like that of a euphoric, mild intoxicant. It wasn't something that would seize me and render me powerless. I was in full control, but his enrapture empowered me to "love" and "be loved" in a way that I'm not sure that I'd ever experienced. After nearly six months, it was time to make some serious decisions about moving forward. The relationship ended because of some crucial matters with which I was not willing to compromise. The main two were, starting over with raising small children, and tolerating dual worship practices. We all have our preferences, and arriving back on the dating scene after more than two decades, my preferences are less negotiable. So — needless to say that breaking free from "Drug" was a challenging emotional task.

The big takeaway here is, if you find yourself attracted to or involved with a man and you know there's no viable future, **cut to the chase and move on**. Don't waste precious time allowing it to trickle down the last drop. By then, your patience with him and fondness of him will have terribly diminished, or you will eventually compromise your principles and desires for something that is less valuable. It's always better when you can walk away amiably. Occupy yourself. Invest in yourself by getting active with your hobbies, your gifts, deferred goals, and the things that bring you joy. Ask God to give you strength. He will. I'm a witness that He'll keep you if you want to be kept!

Dating this time around is also intentional, because I'm much more mature. I assess if or how I'm able to fit in someone else's life and vice versa. Yet, although I now have added years of wisdom and experience, I still need God's guidance. It's best to go to God and be specific about what you desire. No matter what it is you're looking for during the dating process, I advise you to be alert and refrain from engaging in the following behaviors:

#1: Being desperate. You don't have to put yourself out there. You can be desirous, yet not desperate. God will make sure you're in the path of the man He designed for you.

#2: Stop looking for a man. What's supposed to happen will happen. You don't have to be on the hunt for anything.

#3: Stop trying to change a man into what you want him to be. No one is above influence, but people are who they are. Accept them where they are.

Get acquainted with yourself – the real you. If you're still looking for the same things in a man that you were looking for 10 years ago, something may be wrong with that idea. As we grow and mature, our priorities, needs and desires change. Be practical about what you want and what you need. There's a difference between desires and needs, and we must be intune with both. Reflect back on your past relationships; how you may have contributed to the demise of them. Are you working on those things? Do you know what they are? With each relationship, there should be a degree of self-development. You should have questions for yourself, and there should be self-improvement. You won't find anything in a relationship that you can't first find in yourself. You are forever attached to yourself, so it's best to learn how to love the person in the mirror before you seek outside affection. Men will be around. Take some time for yourself. Give yourself a break and heal, you deserve that. A lot of women make the mistake of thinking that their sole source of happiness is in a man. No! You have to discover and create your own happiness. A man can only contribute to your happiness. That's it. You have to know who you are, what you want, and what you need; and then you must be able to communicate those things. You have to be specific, and do not compromise on things that you are not willing to live with.

I trust that you have gained enlightenment from these dating considerations and recommendations. They don't have to be implemented in the order that they are presented, but they should definitely *all* be considered. I hope that they will aid in your dating success, and perhaps even save you some time, energy and relationship-bloopers. **Happy dating!**

"It's important to be open and vulnerable. Your heart has to be open. You have to know what core values and mindsets you want in a significant other."

~HEJIRA "COACH HJ" NITOTO

Love After Divorce

By: Hejira "Coach HJ" Nitoto

ingle mothers who are dating have completely different struggles than single women without children. I want to give hope and encouragement to the women who feel discouraged about dating as a single parent. I want women to know, you will find love again. I'm a mother of 6, but when I was dating after separating from a 15-year marriage, I had 4 children. So trust me when I say, love after divorce is possible. You just have to make some adjustments in how you approach dating, believe in the possibility of new love, and have an open heart.

I was 16 years old when I had my first child. That relationship was non existent and he chose not to be involved in my daughter's life at all. I met my ex-husband (who's 6 years older than me) my senior year of high school At the time, I was living with my older brother and his girlfriend and he was completely against me dating an older man until after I turned18. I tried to reason with him but he wouldn't budge. So I packed up and moved out, which automatically put me in the position of being dependent on my ex-husband and his family, who took me in with open arms.

We were both young when we got together. We had another child before we got married when I was 20. I was pretty stable. I finished highschool and enrolled in college, always kept a job, and paid most of the bills. Meanwhile, he was an aspiring rapper and a music producer but didn't have a consistent stable income. One minute he would have a new job, then in the studio and he went back and forth with that for some time. He wasn't progressing in a career. He was making money here and there and when he was in the studio he was there for long hours. Which left me with the burden of full-time parenting. It was unfair. Something had to give. He always made promises of making it big. But that never came to fruition. At some point, he had to come to the conclusion that he was getting too old for that industry. We had four children to raise and care for. He had no fallback plan. At one point he went to nursing school, completed the program, then decided he didn't want to be a nurse. I had goals and he was stuck trying to achieve his dream. I couldn't do it anymore.

My ex-husband was a funny kind man most of the time but when we had disagreements he had anger and control issues. He would keep tabs on me but I never saw it as control because he did everything in a sweet way. Like when he bought me my first pager and he contacted me often throughout the day. That turned into him telling me what I could and couldn't wear and who I could and couldn't hang out with. He also had a bad temper when things weren't going his way. At one point in our marriage, everything was so rocky between us that we agreed to attend marriage counseling. During counseling, we decided we were going to do better. We were still committed. After counseling, we planned my next pregnancy, bought a home, had a couple of dogs, and he was working a consistent job at Time Warner Cable. He enjoyed his job. We were living the "American Dream". But life took a turn for the worse. Things at work weren't going well and so he went out on stress leave. Then finances became an issue. A short while later, I found my passion in health and fitness and I wanted him to support me. I wanted him to be a part of this lifestyle with me. But everything became about growing his production studio and music career. Honestly, we were growing apart and I felt guilty for a long time. I felt selfish for wanting more and my willingness to sacrifice our family to get it.

Over the years, a lot of things transpired that caused me to lose respect for him. I can take ownership for the lack of communication in our relationship. I knew I needed to work on that. When I lost my respect for him, I only knew of one way to empower myself, and that was to disrespect him. That only made things worse and it became a vicious cycle we couldn't figure out. He resented me for treating him poorly but I was only treating him that way as a result of how he was treating me. It was never-ending. We got into a pattern of seeing who could be more demeaning. Once that started, everything began to deteriorate; the friendship, the marriage, the love. Our marriage became a place of familiarity and contentment rather than love and friendship. We didn't even like each other anymore. I should've ended the marriage many years before I did but I never had the courage to do so. We stayed together for our children. Not only that, I was out to prove that I made the right decision when I left my family at 17 years old to be with him. I didn't want anyone to have the ability to say, *'I told you so.'* I thought it was best to stay and figure it out.

I think he's a good man and tries his best at fatherhood but he doesn't fulfill the adult version of me. I have love and respect for him as a friend and a co-parent. However, we'd come to a point where our personalities were no longer cohesive. He felt like I should've stayed in the marriage and I felt I did all I could to make the marriage work. I was becoming a new person and he couldn't satisfy my needs. I wanted change and he was stuck in his ways of doing things. Even if he was open to changing to meet my needs, I don't think that the person he is would allow it. He'd have to become a different person. We needed balance and we didn't have that. He was able to provide but unable to be as involved with the kids as I was. I felt like that was unfair considering I had my own career as well. I wasn't getting any help and I was way past tired of that. I needed a partner and not another child to parent. Granted, he didn't have a healthy example of what love is and what a healthy relationship looked like. We had plenty of time together for him to figure that out. Looking back there were a lot of red flags in my previous marriage that I wasn't mature enough to notice. He guided me a lot. I was a little girl when we met and started dating so I went along with everything he wanted. Then I grew up.

After the split, my ex-husband was the one that moved out. We agreed that he would still pay certain bills in the house. But that stopped because financially, he was unable to manage taking care of us and himself. We were both laid off and lost our house due to foreclosure. I had to transition quickly. I'd gotten a job and did the best I could managing my single life and keeping the kids' lives as normal as possible. I'd submerged myself in my fitness and I was feeling myself. I was training for a figure competition and that's how I kept myself busy. I was newly single and wanted to experience the single life. Yet, all of my friends were married with children and weren't able or willing to entertain clubs. So I ended up with a group of friends that were much younger than me to hang out with. I was finally able to make decisions for myself without having anyone to answer to. It was empowering as a woman. I was able to do what I wanted to do, freely. I don't believe I gave myself enough time to mourn the loss of my marriage, which

I think is important. I felt fine and it was on to the next. Besides that, I didn't want my children to see me struggling. The divorce was hard enough on them.

My oldest son began getting into trouble at school. He'd gotten caught with marijuana on campus and somehow my ex-husband felt that I was to blame, saying it happened because I wasn't spending enough time with the kids. I was taken aback considering I was a full-time parent and he saw them once maybe twice a week. He made the unilateral decision of taking my son to live with him. I told him that if he was going to take the oldest, then take them all. I came home one day to find that my boys and their belongings were gone. I didn't have the financial or mental means to fight him. I had to focus on packing up our foreclosed house with the help of my current husband and another friend. I left everything I didn't want or didn't have space for in the house and moved into my first apartment I'd rented on my own with little to no help It was one of the most difficult sad times of my life. Yet, I felt liberated.

I'd dated a couple of people in between my ex-husband and my current husband. But I was clear with them that I wasn't looking to be in a relationship. I was just passing time. Dating got old really quickly. I was a mother and I knew I wanted to be a wife again but I wanted someone who was on my level. I needed someone who was willing to co-parent and be a part of raising my children with me. Going from one guy to the next wasn't an option for me.

I met my current husband through the Herbalife business but we were just acquaintances. We ran into one another at an Herbalife event a few months later. I had 4 children, limited time, and was going through a divorce at the time we met so the relationship had no choice but to move slowly. He was younger than me, a bachelor, with no children. He barely had any long-term relationships and neither of us was sure if a relationship was something we wanted or needed. But we kept dating because of the strong physical and mental connection we had developed.

Most of our date nights were spent in the gym or a movie and dinner. We became really good friends during that time. We were intimate but there were no strings attached. Interestingly, he was convinced that my ex-husband and I would reconcile. He didn't see us truly going our separate ways after 15 years of marriage and 4 kids. He confessed that he really liked me but I could see where he was guarded because he didn't want to get his feelings hurt, which was understandable.

I thought I was clear on what I wanted from him and that I was truly done with my marriage. He was looking at it from an outside perspective. However, there was a lot of uncertainty surrounding this *'thing'* he and I had going on. We were just enjoying each other's company. I wasn't sure where he and I were headed. He is 4 years younger than me and we were in completely different places in life. I had a different level of responsibility than he did. I'd been on my own since I was 16 years old, I was married for 15 years, and I had 4 four children. Whereas, he was a college athlete and living the single life. Looking at me, I was a ready-made family and he wasn't sure he was ready, nor was I.

As a woman who was older than him and a little more mature, I had to teach him a lot of things about life. Our life structures were very different but he was open to learning as I was open to teaching. Don't get me wrong, he's not perfect and I did notice some red flags. He wasn't stable when we began dating. He didn't have a place of his own. He'd stay between LA and the Bay Area with his sister and his friends. He also didn't have a car. He didn't have good credit. But I loved who he was as a family man. Those were minor issues that could be fixed. We all grow up differently and everyone needs time to evolve into adulthood. The red flags I saw weren't worth me throwing a good man away.

He wanted to be a family man. His parents were never married but his father was very active in his life. He wanted something different than what he saw growing up. Although both his parents were present, he wanted to make sure his children didn't have the same experience as he did. As far as relationships go, he didn't want to mimic his father's behavior. Once he sets his mind to something, he is great with following through. I respect that about him. His actions match his words.

After a while, I'd come to a point where the relationship was getting confusing for me. We either had to move forward together or I had to move on from him, alone. I'd met his siblings and his father while we were dating but I didn't meet his mother until after I was divorced. That was also when I knew that he felt differently about our situation and learned he was seeing other people, which hurt my feelings. But I really couldn't say anything because we weren't in a committed relationship. He asked about my divorce regularly. He seemed to want to know if the filing was complete, etc. I always assured him that everything was moving in a forward direction. After everything was finalized, I was able to fully focus on the new life I was creating. About a year and a half in, he decided that he wanted to take our relationship to the next level.

He met my children 6 months into dating. I was a stay-at-home mom and my youngest, who was 2 years old at the time, was with me a lot. So he spent a lot of time with my youngest child. Due to that, they became close. During our courtship, he did reveal to me that he'd been in a previous relationship with a woman who had a daughter and he developed a relationship with her daughter. He said he stayed in the relationship longer than he wanted to because of the little girl but the split was difficult when it did happen because he lost his access to the child. So I understood his reservations with me.

While my husband and I were dating, we had a serious conversation about children. I was done having children. *At least, I thought I was.* Probably about 4 months into our relationship, he came to me and told me he wanted to have 3 children of his own. I thought, *WHAT?!?* I asked him if he was taking into account my children. He said, no, he wanted 3 children of his own and if I wasn't willing to have 3 more children, maybe we shouldn't move forward. I was beyond shocked. I gave it some thought and I told him I was willing to have more children for him. Deep down, I was hoping one child would be sufficient. Later into our relationship, he told me that was his attempt to scare me off. At that time, he was still in the mindset that I would get back with my husband. He didn't want to be the one to break things off. He was hoping I'd be the one to do it. He was self-sabotaging.

The interaction between him and my children was important to me. My oldest children witnessed me and my ex-husband as a unit so they were used to that dynamic. The divorce was hard on them and they were standoffish with my current husband while we were dating. But with time to process the new normal and pacing ourselves, the kids were able to adjust. There were also incidents that happened that opened the window for trust and vulnerability between him and my older children. At the start of our relationship, my daughter had just gone off to college. I wasn't the kind of parent that called and checked on her a lot or asked about her feelings. My thinking was, 'if she needs me she'll call me.' I was treating her like she was an adult. She was having the college experience which wasn't something I was privy to. Yet, he was. He'd been to college and lived that life so he could relate to her. I appreciated that and it made me fall in love with him more.

My third child was 5 years old at the time and my husband probably had the hardest time with him. They're close now, but he took the divorce between his father and I the hardest. He tested the boundaries. He wanted to make sure my husband knew he wasn't his daddy. That relationship took time.

I knew he was good with children based on the interaction between him and his nephew and nieces. After seeing that, I knew I wanted to be the mother of this man's children. I was getting close to the end of my 30's and I vowed to myself that I wasn't going to have any more children once I reached 40. So I told him that there was no pressure but we needed to plan for children sooner rather than later. About 6-9 months into us being fully committed, I got pregnant with our first daughter.

We moved in together when I got pregnant and he immediately became a third party to the co-parenting between my ex-husband and I. I have to say, he was great with my kids. He took their school work very seriously and spent a lot of time helping them with their school work and building an open honest relationship with each of them. He taught one of my sons how to ride a bike. The transition was fairly smooth, considering. Even my ex-husband was accepting of my new husband even when he was just my boyfriend. They have mutual respect for each other's role in the kids' lives.

After the birth of our first daughter, he and I agreed to try for another child. Little did he know, I was going to try to get this over with. I got pregnant again 15 months later. He is an amazing father and stepfather (bonus dad). We'd talked about marriage and I was coming to a point where I felt like that was necessary. I didn't like the idea of *'playing house,'* when you're living together and having children but not actually married. He and I discussed marriage early in our relationship. He had a different stance. Marriage wasn't important to him. He felt like it was just a piece of paper. But he was open to getting married if marriage was important to his partner. My thoughts were opposing. I'd been married before so I knew what marriage entailed. I also didn't agree that marriage was just a legality. I felt like it was a mindset. I also wanted to set, what I felt, was the right example for my children. I think two people that are doing life together, should be married.

Every time I mentioned marriage he was nonchalant about it like, *yea yea, we'll get to it*. Eventually, he came to me and revealed that he wanted a big wedding which wasn't what I wanted because I'd already experienced that with my first husband. I didn't want to spend that kind of money on a wedding.

One night when we were sitting in bed, he told me that this was the year we were going to get married. We wrote out a guest list and everything. I suggested that we go to City Hall to get married and plan for a big wedding later. At this time we weren't even engaged, we were just having discussions about what we wanted. One day, I received a random email from a film agency looking for couples who wanted to get married on March 17, 2020, for their show. They said they'd provide a venue among other things. I showed him the email and we both thought it was interesting but brushed it off. Then it came up in conversation again. I told him maybe we should apply. He agreed. So we applied and were accepted! March 17, 2020, was supposed to be the big day. But due to the weather, the date was pushed back to March 24th. I suggested that we should do a small, intimate wedding with just the kids and our siblings just in case things didn't work out as planned. So that's what we did.

On March 14th, I had a girls brunch with my girlfriends and my daughter. After brunch, we went to the spa and he showed up in a suit with the kids and proposed. It was 3 days before the wedding. We rented a small space in downtown LA and hired a photographer. My siblings, his sister, and our children were in attendance. It was the perfect ceremony. Covid-19 was on the rise and we suspected there would be problems. However, everything was still set for the 24th and we hoped for the best. They had stipulations to their arrangement. We were unable to invite guests and we had to purchase our own attire. I bought a dress and he rented a tuxedo. Just as we suspected, due to Covid-19, the show was being pushed back yet again. We recently received a call from the show saying they anticipated picking everything back up in July or August and wanted to know if we were still interested. I told them, "we got married on March 17th."

As I stated previously, he didn't value marriage. Now that we're married, I can see a shift in his behavior and attitude. He's enjoying being married. He's carrying himself differently. Although he had opposing views of marriage than me, and I had to wait for him to come around, I knew he was a genuine person. That attracted me to him. He's very family-oriented and I love that about him. I was able to witness those qualities in him while we were dating and I knew he was the one I wanted to hold on to. We turned out to be everything I thought we would be. I can truly say that 6 years removed from my divorce, my life and my children's lives have been better since.

It's important to be open and vulnerable. Your heart has to be open. You have to know what core values and mindsets you want in a significant other. When I met my current husband, I knew early on that his thought process was in alignment with what I wanted. I was fortunate to meet someone with my husband's qualifications. I think there's a fine line between having standards and being flexible. A mature woman has to sit down and write out what's truly important in a mate and what you're willing to compromise. I was clear on my goals and what I wanted and I got just that.

Be open to:

- trying new things
- having your feelings hurt
- someone you might not be traditionally attracted to

I didn't know what the new package was going to look like. Oftentimes, we have this idea in our heads of what our lives and partners will look like. That closes us off to new experiences and exciting outcomes. **Have fun and go with the flow!** Don't put any pressure on anyone. Trust your heart. Listen to your gut. Do their actions meet their words? Does yours? Focus on your well-being and that of your children. The right person will come along, **I promise.**

"Ladies and Gentlemen, STOP thinking you can dodge the process of building a healthy, loving relationship with another person without first working on you!"

~ ELAM B. KING

UnReal Love

By: Elam B. King

When I was a young man, I thought like a young man. Nothing mattered to me but making money, looking good, my friends, and sleeping with beautiful women. Now that I'm a man and I know who I am and the direction I want my life to go in, I'm a lot more grounded. I'm able to see the error of not only someone else's ways but my own. As I've grown, my needs have changed. My desires have changed and the way I view myself has changed. When I was in my 20's I was moving through life carelessly and so were the women that I was sleeping with. I had to undergo a serious identity shift to understand love and relationships. Now that the women have spoken, it's my turn.

I was young, fresh out of college, and working a lot. I had a job in corporate america and the work was consuming. I worked a shift from 3-11p, sometimes doing overtime in the mornings, and occasional weekends. When you spend that kind of time at work, you begin to see people differently. Slowly, you get the drunk effect whereas your co-workers start becoming more appealing to you due to constant interaction and visibility.

It was 2000, I was clean-cut and well-dressed. At the time, I was still hanging out with my frat brothers and all the friends I'd built strong relationships with during college. So I wasn't socializing at my job very much. When I was promoted to a management role, there was some talk about me not hanging out with the staff in the office. They felt like I wasn't taking the initiative to get to know everyone. So I tried to immerse myself into the corporate world, that's when I met Nadia.

One night while we were all at the club having a good time, Nadia approached me. She said, "Do you like girls?" Odd question, right? She asked me that because I didn't really pay the women at my job any mind. I'd just spent 4 years at Hampton University where I met and slept with some of the finest women and being around that environment spoiled me. Coming out of college and getting a job placed me in the real world but mentally I was still looking for the type of woman I was in college with. Most of the women at my job were average, in my opinion and didn't measure up. I didn't realize that anyone noticed my disinterest for the women at work. I didn't even notice my disinterest was noticeable. Nadia told me that I walked around with an "I'm all that" attitude. I could tell she thought I was all that. What she didn't know was I was sleeping with other women at the job but I kept everything as discreet as possible. The last thing I needed was drama at the job.

When she asked the question, do I like girls? I wasn't offended, I simply told her, "give me your phone number and you'll find out." I can't say I noticed her before she approached me. Had she never approached me, I would never have said anything to her. I'd seen her before but her team was on one side of the building and mine was on the other. Even when I arrived to work, my team was located near the entrance so I didn't have too much of a need to see and socialize with the other teams. Nadia was used to attention from men. But to be honest, she was a beautiful woman, but initially she wasn't necessarily my type.

Little did I know, that interaction with her was going to shape the next 20 years of my life. Nadia and I began having sex. She was 31 years old and I was 25 years old. We were sleeping together for 2 years before she got pregnant. We used condoms occasionally and she was off and on with birth control pills. I never even thought to have a conversation with her about making sure she was taking birth control because she wasn't someone I was looking to go further with. Nadia got pregnant with my son at the time she was seeing someone else and I was sleeping with someone else. When Nadia called me to tell me she was pregnant, I conveniently used the fact that she was seeing someone else against her. I tried to convince her that I wasn't too trusting that the baby was mine. She insisted that she wasn't sleeping with anyone but me. She was expressing that she was pregnant and that she was committing to me. Meanwhile I was using whatever I could to remove myself from a commitment.

At the time everything in my life was pretty well aligned. Nadia and I were good friends, she was cute, the sex was good, and my finances were in place. I felt like I could make everything work. I didn't know about pre-marital counseling, generational curses, love languages, and other key tools that can promote a lasting relationship. Some men choose women for who they are in the moment when we have no relationship direction, not for who they're going to be in the future. Some women choose men for who they're going to be and now I know that Nadia was choosing me for who I was going to be in the future. During the course of the pregnancy, I had to decide what I was going to do. I looked to my baseline, which was God first, and the man and woman being in one home when they have a child. I figured she was a good candidate for marriage and I could handle the situation.

When I met Nadia, she was a single mother with 2 children. Their biological father was intermittently present in their lives. When I first met Nadia, I didn't care that she was a single mother because we were just having sex and I wasn't trying to be a father nor a stepfather. Her kids were about 3 and 4 years old when Nadia and I started sleeping together. I had every intention of being a present father for my son when he was born, but what about these other two children? I figured I may as well make it work with Nadia because she had my son. I grew up with both my parents in the home and I wanted to give my son the same environment. When my parents asked me, "why her?" I told them that I didn't want her kids to grow up with no father at all when I had the love and resources to give. I genuinely wanted to be a father to her other 2 children.

When my son was born, I fell in love with him. I fell in love with everything attached to my son. Nadia was attached to him because she was his mother. I cared about her, yes, but that's what happens when men are out here sleeping around. They run into someone they care about and they do "fall in love." I thought I'd fallen in love with Nadia. But the truth is, at the time she and I began a sexual relationship, I didn't know myself as a man. I thought this thing I had going on with her must be love because I was truly in love with the kids. I can look back now and see that it wasn't love between Nadia and I. There was a lot of sexual chemistry but it wasn't love. I was making a decision to be with her but the decision wasn't driven based on how I felt about her.

When you're out here dating, it's important that a man is the one making the decision to commit. Not that a woman is influencing a man to commit. Although you can never know what goes on inside the mind of another human being, there are behaviors that you'll witness when you know a man is looking to commit to you. For starters, he'll start becoming the leader. He'll give direction or he'll share his future plans with you. He'll introduce you to his parents. When he starts making decisions that include you in his vision, that's a tell-tale sign that a man wants you long term.

On the other hand, if a man is not trying to fit you into his world and he's making sure the division is clear, he doesn't see you in his future. More than likely, he's only looking to pull you into his bed and that's where the confusion comes in. For a man, bringing a woman into the bedroom and bringing a woman into his world are two completely different events. It looks similar. And a man may bring a woman to a gathering with his cousins and friends there and his mother *might* show up. But because you think he brought you around his family, you're automatically inclined to have sex with him and commit to him. The woman assumes that this means there's a commitment coming. Sometimes men will create the illusion that it's more than what it is. You have to be mindful of when a man is trying to keep you on the hook. Listen to what he's saying and watch what he's doing.

After my son was born in 2001, Nadia and I broke up a few times. We both left our jobs independently. She then moved to Atlanta and I attempted to get away from her by moving to Florida. But my love for my son kept bringing us back together. My son had gotten sick a few times while we were broken up. That brought me around a lot more. I had to be there for my son but being with him means being around his mother. The more that went on, the more I began to persuade myself into believing being with Nadia wouldn't be a bad idea.

Had Nadia been paying attention or been in the right place to pay attention she would've seen my wayward ways. She would've seen that I was a paper chaser but I wasn't good with money. She would've seen that I wasn't going to church and being spiritually guided because she was laying next to me on Sunday mornings. She would've seen that I wasn't that close with some of my family members because I wasn't visiting them often.

Before a woman makes a determination about a man or wants to involve herself in a committed relationship, ask yourself this, *'what is my direction and purpose in life?'* At that point, a woman can decide whether or not a man fits into *her* life. You're doing the picking, you're not being picked. When you know what you want and what direction your life is going in, the law of attraction is in effect. God will make sure that person is somewhere in your circle. The trick is, you have to be in a position to pick. When you're where you want to be in life, only then can you pick the best person for you. There is no question to ask a man that will give you magic answers to be with a man. The answers are in his behavior. Ask yourself the right questions based on your expectations. It's not about asking him the right questions, it's about asking yourself the right questions. The only mind that you have the opportunity to control is your own. You cannot control another person's mind.

Also, women need to make sure they have their own life plan and make sure that a man fits into the direction your life is going in as well. Usually, when a woman is sleeping around and becomes pregnant she'll become fixated on capturing a specific man, forgetting her own life goals. She becomes consumed with getting a man to settle down with her. A woman shouldn't compromise expectations and her life's direction just because she's gotten pregnant. Make sure that a man has the characteristics of someone you truly want to be with. When you're grounded in this way, whether or not you get pregnant, you won't get caught up. Especially in someone who you know you wouldn't be with long term otherwise. You'll be able to look at the situation for face value instead of trying to make a relationship that doesn't suit you, work in your favor just due to the pregnancy. Relationships don't work that way. That's when everything goes left. We don't realize that if the relationship isn't going to work, a child in the equation won't change that.

One day while I was leaving Nadia's place, she stopped me because she wanted to tell me something. I noticed she was acting childlike and giddy. She said she was going to say what she needed to say and shut the door. So I stood there waiting. She went on to tell me she loved me and closed the door after she said it. I thought to myself, "*Oh shit, here we go.*" I left and went home. I began saying 'I love you' back to her because I didn't want her to feel stupid. Men are conditioned in many ways to give women the response they're looking for just to avoid hurting their feelings.

Oftentimes, men will lead women on for many different reasons. It could be ego-driven. It could be that he knows he has a grip on a good woman and he wants to keep her around until he knows what he wants to do with his life. Maybe he really does like you but doesn't know what he wants to do with you because he doesn't have himself figured out. In a situation like that, a woman has to decide if she's going to stick around while he figures himself out. Should she choose to stay, she must also be okay and not feel played if he doesn't choose to be with her. Once you know that you and a man aren't on the same page, the decision is on you.

Women normally have a plan when it comes to relationships and men don't. I had no plans of being with Nadia in any other capacity than what we already were. She seemed to have a plan and I didn't. I can't say she trapped me, I don't know. That's more of a question for her to answer. One time, my son asked me, "if mom hadn't gotten pregnant, would you have married her?" I told him, "I don't know." At the moment, I hadn't given it much thought. Since then, I've discovered the truth is I probably wouldn't have been with her long term if it wasn't for our son.

My son was born in 2001 and we got married in 2003. Somewhere along the line Nadia and I began having intimacy issues. I was unable to get what I needed from her so I went looking elsewhere. The woman I was cheating on my wife with, was also a single mother when we met. I met the other woman, Victoria, while at work in a call center. At the time I was working for Atlantic Central and when Hurricane Katrina hit, some of their employees relocated to our call center. To be clear, I never lied to Victoria about my marriage. Everyone knew I was married and who I was married to because my wife worked for Atlantic Central as well. Victoria and I were in the same training class, that's when we began getting to know each other. I wasn't trying to be wild. But I had needs that I couldn't ignore. I needed sex. I needed intimacy.

Women and men are typically taught the exact opposite of the virtue of self. Most women are taught from a young age to have morals and values, don't sleep around, be careful who you're giving yourself to, etc. Women are taught to value their bodies. Men, however, are taught the exact opposite of that. We're taught to sleep around before we settle down. We're taught to be promiscuous. It's okay for us to date multiple women. Essentially we are taught a concept that devalues the penis. Although, the penis and the vagina are equally valuable.

I grew up with a lot of freedom. My father gave me condoms when I was 12/13 years old. I wasn't having sex at those ages but I had the freedom to do so if I wanted to. Neither of my parents cared if I was sexually active. In fact, my father promoted it. That left me with the idea that I can and should sleep around. So I did. Now that I see the ramifications of sex, I urge women and men to be more selective in whom they're sharing themselves with.

There are men who know their way around a woman's body and that can be a gift and a curse. When a man starts giving a woman orgasms and intimacy, a bond is forming. You have to be careful because this is how attachments are born. Overall, the controller of the temple is the individual. Only you can control what happens with your body. Women need to remember that they have the option of saying yes or no to sex. If women want men to stop having casual sex with and impregnating them before truly loving them, then you have to be more selective in who you're choosing to give your body to. If you're looking to get yours and move on then by all means, do that. But if you're dating with the intent of a lasting relationship, you have to learn how to weed out the good and the bad before you sleep with them.

I didn't take notice of the things I didn't like about Nadia until after we'd gotten married. I also didn't understand the concept of intention until after I married her. In the beginning, I met her representative; the person she wanted me to see. She showed up this way for so long that I was unable to see her flaws. After we said 'I do,' I saw a lot more of the real side of her. I began to understand who she truly was. Simultaneously, I was doing a lot of self-discovering. That's the dangerous part of getting into a committed relationship or marriage before you've discovered yourself. You may have created this life that you think you want or that you're trying to make work, but when you wake up to who you really are, you may discover that you've made some life-changing decisions prematurely.

When I began to see Nadia in her element, I saw some things about her that repulsed me.. Understand this, whatever it took to get your significant other is what you need to do to keep them. You can't stop doing those things when you think you have a person hooked. You have to do your due diligence before marrying someone. Make sure you know exactly what it is you're getting yourself into. If you don't, you'll regret it and feel a sense of guilt for letting yourself down. I walked into marriage not understanding the sanctity of marriage and what it takes for both parties to truly be committed.

While Nadia and I were dating, I felt like a priority for her. There was not a time when she didn't fit my needs in. Once I said, 'I do.' all of that was over. Often, people that are dating with children live through the infamous 'honeymoon phase' of the relationship. This phase is where you encounter your partner's representative, then you may get married and meet the "real" person. When the honeymoon phase wears off and you're left with routine life and children, you'll be biologically drawn to constantly caring for the children and forgetting about your spouse; slipping into a life of parenting with your spouse not being married to them. This is how resentment builds and love fades. This also opens the door for cheating or divorce.

Looking back, I wish I had a mentor when I decided to be a father to her two children, that way, I could've been better prepared for some of the obstacles we'd faced. I wished I'd reached out for help when I needed the guidance. I feel like I shorted my children because I didn't know some important things about myself for at least the first ten years of my marriage. My self-discovery journey came after all the life-altering decisions I made. A lot of times, I was moreso a part of the problem rather than the solution. I thought I knew what I was doing and I didn't.

If I could go back and give my younger self some advice, I'd say, be honest and upfront with women about where you stand. Doing this diminishes all confusion and opens the door for honest communication. This also gives the woman the opportunity to decide whether or not getting involved with you is a good idea for her, rather than robbing her of the ability to make an informed decision. Giving a woman the truth, even though it may or may not be favorable to them, provides them with the security of truth. You may not be in her bed, but she trusts that you're going to be honest with her. It's difficult for some men to grasp this concept because we're taught to avoid communication. We believe that if we tell women the truth, we'll lose them, and that's the wrong way to view the effects of telling the truth.

Here are 3 Things I'd Suggest Single Mothers STOP Doing:

#1: Ladies, stop just falling in love with a man. Be more intentional about your dating practices. Once you establish your expectations in life, you should begin living that way. There's nothing wrong with dating but before you decide to commit yourself to someone, allow yourself to get attached to someone or get physically intimate with them, know what you want, and don't compromise for *any* man. Figure out what your non-negotiables are and make them known. This helps the flow of the relationship. When you know what a person's expectations are, then you know how to move forward and fulfill that person's needs.

The reason for this is that if you do not walk with intention, then you can run the risk of letting life circumstances dictate how you want to move forward. Sometimes it can be a baby, and sometimes people begin to commit to moving in together too soon, sometimes it can be because you've just been together for so long, you just push forward into marriage without doing the due diligence of yourself and making the proper choice of who you commit long term to.

You fall into something when you don't see it. Although the concept of "falling in love" may sound romantic, falling in love is dangerous. Allowing yourself to love someone based on self-awareness and understanding of the other person is intentional and sets you up for a better level of success in your relationship.

#2: Stop being afraid of letting go of a man if he's not meeting your needs or living up to your expectations within the relationship. There's no winning in staying in a relationship that is one-sided just because you like a man or you're afraid of being alone. At the point you notice that there's no direction with the relationship, STOP HAVING SEX WITH HIM! You can still hang out and enjoy each other's company. But I repeat, DO. NOT. HAVE. SEX. WITH. HIM. If you continue having sex with him, you'll find yourself in a perpetual state of yearning for this person. Sex is a very powerful, energetic, highly emotional act that results in attachments. At that point, you won't be able to make decisions in your own best interest nor the interest of your children. If you think continuing to have sex and avoiding the necessary conversations will work out best for you, and you believe that the problem will fix itself, it most likely won't.

#3: Listen to that sixth sense that alerts you to the people in your surroundings. Trust your own instincts in the beginning and act on them quickly. Don't wait. I believe most women know who is and isn't good for them. But some just ignore the truth because some always want what they can't have. If you think you want someone, talk to them about it. Even if you get your feelings hurt by hearing answers you don't like, at least you know the truth and who you're dealing with. It's better to know than to wonder. If a man lets you know that he doesn't want to be with you, then leave him immediately. Don't wait and stop trying to convince him that you're the best option. Don't allow him to smooth you over and keep you on the hook either. You also have to be mature enough to have an open, honest, and direct dialogue about the direction of the relationship. If he cannot do that, then stop committing your body, mind, and your emotions to this man. Don't allow yourself to be in the position to get picked but instead lean back and seek to create an environment that allows for a man to come forward with a proposition for a relationship with you.

I've noticed that women that have kids have a tendency to evaluate the man they're dating for their children before assessing whether or not he works for her as a woman. Single mothers tend to inadvertently put their children's needs before their own. When it comes to dating, that definitely shouldn't be the case.

When it comes to disciplining children, single mothers need to have that conversation with a man before becoming committed to him. It's also a conversation that should be ongoing. Everyone's style of discipline is different and you should iron out the do's/don'ts because the wrong way of disciplining another person's child can cause problems and/or end the relationship. Ladies, don't get with someone who you feel doesn't have what it takes to parent your child properly. I never viewed Nadia's children as my 'stepkids.' They were also my kids and I tried to raise them the same but we ran into challenges with our individual parenting styles. Men going into relationships with single mothers should avoid the single mother who doesn't trust your ability to lead her and the children in the right direction. If she wants to maintain control and not release the children to you, you will experience some parenting challenges.

A single mother has to be able to understand the man's role in the house. He's a man/leader and a father/leader. Those are two separate categories. Women have to be more mature about having these conversations. Women should crown the man King of the house because if you choose the right man for you, then that should be the way he's viewed. How she treats him will influence the children to treat him the same. Only the woman can set that tone. As a woman, when you say 'I do,' you are really saying 'I will do.' It takes a lot of accountability to be a wife; a woman that keeps the environment with her family steady and comfortable. If a woman hasn't paid attention to a man and doesn't know or understand what his expectations are before marrying him, you may find yourself saying, 'this is too much' when you actually get married and that's partially because you walked into the marriage blindly.

Stop believing you have to put yourself out there so someone can find you. When you're walking in your purpose, God will send him. The same rules apply to men. We all have to stop being afraid to be alone. We all want love. We want to have the best possible results in a relationship with someone that desires, respects, and honors us inside and out. You can have that, but you have to start with you. Stop thinking that you can dodge the process of building a healthy, loving relationship with another person, without first working on you. It's not just about fitness or changing your hairstyle, but it's about embarking on a deep self-discovery journey. Being in "your prime" isn't about your age. You're in your prime when you **know** who you are, you **accept** who you are, and you **love** who you are becoming.

Conclusion

I am so excited about the abundance of love that is about to enter into your world! To be able to share the many stories to help assure you that there is pure hope in dating with purpose, is rewarding.

I would like to press upon you the importance of self-love, self-awareness, and inner happiness. You must have these things first before taking on a relationship on whether you are a single mom or not. That means you need to press more in these areas as a single mom or if you're dating the single mom.

Schedule out your time. Time with God and self, time with kids, and time to date, intentionally.

With this new perspective, I had to really take these things into serious consideration and take immediate action while dating with children. So as I began to start my journey to date, I was very careful about where I put my energy and my environment. Casually dating was no longer an option for me. I had to stand in that truth and make that clear with the men I was collecting data from.

I began putting myself around positive, loving couples, and ironically a few of my mentors were successfully married couples.

Create the space and visualize how you see yourself living. I saw myself living in a thriving marriage. Although I began to attract all different types of men in my life, the moment I shifted my thinking and embraced the change as to WHY I was dating, more qualified bachelors started to show up, allowing me to have healthy options, which led to the right one finding me.

I had to be more specific about what I wanted in the man I would date and possibly marry. I knew I wanted a man who not only loved God, but was God-fearing. He had to be a father as well, a loving, responsible father. I knew I wanted a man that was stable mentally and emotionally as well as financially. Communication, respect, loyalty, and integrity are all key factors. He has to have and take responsibility on his own, no mama's boys. A man that is not scared of being vulnerable is very important, too. These are some of the core things that I have on my list. It is very vital to have standards and set boundaries, and above all, honor your own standards and boundaries.

Be specific about what you want. Do I expect perfection, **NO**. We all are flawed. Just know what you want and know what you will be willing to work through. I always say, 'we have to make sure our crazies align or we will be experiencing the same crap just from a different toilet.' **That's never fun.**

INVALUABLE TIPS to DATING with PURPOSE

- **Build yourself up spiritually**
- **Learn how to love yourself again**
- **Trust yourself**
- **Date yourself**
- **Embrace your flaws, communicate your flaws**
- **Define what you want**
- **Start a personal growth regimen**
- **Receive mentorship by those successfully living the life you desire (e.g. successful marriages), which changed my view towards men, money, and marriage**
- **Seek Counseling**
- **Give yourself adequate time to heal from long term emotional damage (1-year minimum)**
- **Focus on children and don't lose sight of their needs and growth**
- **Focus on your overall health, wellness, and fitness**
- **Become limitless, change your belief system to a positive one and speak affirmations**
- **Set timelines and goals as to when you will date again**
- **Make a list of key traits/qualities that you want in your PURPOSE PARTNER**
- **Stand in your truth (healthy truth)**

- **Honor and respect your standards (create your standards within reason)**
- **Set Boundaries**
- **Make sure he/she aligns with all of the above**

I am so incredibly grateful! I am now happily dating again with a healthier mindset. I am now operating in wholeness, and I am much more in tune with my inner me. **I enjoy collecting data.**

Thank you for taking the time to invest in yourself and supporting me with my single moms movement to create healthy change. Thank you for taking the time to read through this amazing tool. My goal is that something or many things resonated with you, so much so that your life will be forever changed, and you are that much closer, if not already, to finding **YOUR PURPOSE PARTNER.**

About the Authors

Tona Phillips is a College Instructor at The Universal College of Beauty, Inglewood, CA and Master Cosmetologist serving Greater Los Angeles. As the single mom to one amazing daughter, she is passionate about helping men and women engage in self-awareness and self-love.

Taina Anthony is a competitive athlete, a successful entrepreneur, and a mom of four amazing children while attaining a dual degree in Business and Accounting. As the CEO of *"Gettyefit"*, a wellness consulting firm, her mission supports the alignment of the mind, body, and soul through nutrition, health, and fitness coaching. *Taina* is also the Founder of *Naturally Sophisticated Women*, a nonprofit organization dedicated to bringing women together to empower one other while embracing their healthy living journey.

Ina Mekesha, born in Delhi, LA is the mother of two wonderful young men, ages 21 and 19. As a paraprofessional with the Clark County School District for 25 years, the Las Vegas, Nevada resident is also the CEO of a notable credit restoration business. Ina Mekesha is passionate about teaching at-risk youth life skills and financial literacy. She also enjoys working out and learning new ways to live a healthier lifestyle.

Shi Ciron, the 30 something single mother of one beautiful pre-teen daughter, is a native of Milwaukee, WI. As an energetic, Serial Entrepreneur navigates the deep waters of dating, she continues to put God first in everything she does. Her purpose in life is to help women choose themselves first and make inner healing a priority.

Ajeya Hongo is a Mother, a financial Coach & Network Marketing Professional who used all trials and tribulations that life gave her and turned it into **POWER**.

Dr. Earleen Parson Ross is the CEO of ER Publishing and Founder of **Distinguished D.I.V.A.s** — Daughters of Integrity, Virtue, and Authority, a mentorship program for adolescent girls (11-18yrs). Dr. Ross is a champion of women and girls coaching them to maturity in womanhood in mind, body, and soul. Dr. Parson Ross is the proud mother of two amazing children, Cortney and Patrick Aaron.

Hejira "Coach HJ" Nitoto is a certified personal trainer, NPC figure competitor, and fit mother of 6 awesome children. Her purpose is to help people who are serious about living a sustainable healthier happier lifestyle; especially women and mothers.

Elam B. King, a New Jersey native, attended Hampton University, graduating with a B.S. in Marketing. He later obtained 2 MBA's, while managing a family, pursuing a rewarding career in sales, and serving in the community with the Stone Mountain-Lithonia chapter of Kappa Alpha Psi Fraternity, Inc. Elam's personal mission is to help individuals cultivate fulfilled lives of intention and accountability. This proud father of six amazing children also loves spending time growing his vegetable and fruit garden.

Ayesha Goodall is an author, speaker, and wellness expert from Los Angeles, California. With a professional background in Psychology, she has embraced an indestructible passion to empower others through her signature brand, "ZenFit w/Coach Eesh," which promotes mind & body connectivity to fitness & nutrition.

As a Supermom of three, Ayesha has the pleasure of balancing single motherhood as she empowers other single moms worldwide to embrace their power and walk in their purpose with her incredible philanthropic foundation, "Repairing Roses."

"EMPOWER. ENLIGHTEN. ELEVATE." is this fearless entrepreneur's mantra as she transforms the minds of her audience.